refresh your prayers

uncommon
devotions
to restore
power and praise

Lori Hatcher

Through captivating storytelling, Lori Hatcher escorts the reader on a 60-day journey to unpack God's truth on the purpose and power of prayer. She masterfully tackles the questions we wrestle with about prayer and invites us to renew our souls through deeper intimacy with Him. Whether you're a new or mature Christ-follower, you won't be disappointed.

—**LESLIE BENNETT,** director of Women's Ministry Initiatives, Revive Our Hearts

Rejuvenate your prayer life. Hatcher offers encouragement to those of us who've hit dull spots in our spiritual fervor.

—**CECIL MURPHEY,** author or coauthor of 140 books, including *Gifted Hands: The Ben Carson Story* and *90 Minutes in Heaven*

From the first chapter to the very last, *Refresh Your Prayers* spawned in me an unexpected craving for something I hadn't felt in a long time. . . . In her unique, God-inspired way, Lori helped me to realize the preciousness of every moment I spend sharing my heart with God and listening for His voice. Thank you, Lori, for investing your time and energy to create this gem that will rouse us from our sleepy prayer lives into that sacred space called His Presence.

—**DEBBIE WATFORD,** pastor's wife and former director of Lay Servant Ministries

Lori does a wonderful job of creating a devotional that is both Bible-based and life-centered. She teaches us to balance the supreme sovereignty of God in planning and directing our lives with the responsibility we have to ask, appeal, and cry out to God. She maintains an excellent balance of theological truth about prayer and practical ways to live out that truth in daily life. The personally transparent and real-life illustrations are very moving. I've used many daily prayer devotionals, but this one will continue to guide my prayer life.

—**STEVE BRADLEY,** retired professor and administrator, Columbia International University; engineer, pastor, and missionary

Lori Hatcher's devotions in *Refresh Your Prayers* help both new and long-time believers examine their assumptions about prayer, God's role, and God's expectations of a praying believer. Using biblical texts and personal experience, Hatcher explores common attitudes and practices in Christian prayer, leading readers to discover deeper purpose, spiritual richness, and joy in the process.

—**DEBORAH S. DECIANTIS,** PhD, North Greenville University

Refresh Your Prayers will lead you into a creative and meaningful conversation with our heavenly Father that will revolutionize your prayer life.

—**LINDA GILDEN,** author, editor, and speaker

refresh your prayers

uncommon
devotions
to restore
power and praise

Lori Hatcher

Our Daily Bread
Publishing™

Interior design by Faceout Studio, Paul Nielsen

Library of Congress Cataloging-in-Publication Data

Names: Hatcher, Lori, author.
Title: Refresh your prayers : uncommon devotions to restore power and
   praise / Lori Hatcher.
Description: Grand Rapids : Our Daily Bread Publishing, 2022. | Summary:
   "This 60-devotional provides uncommon insights from unusual verses about
   prayer to help readers connect with God in a powerful way"-- Provided by
   publisher.
Identifiers: LCCN 2021045520 | ISBN 9781640701410 (paperback)
Subjects: LCSH: Prayer--Christianity--Miscellanea. | Bible--Meditations. |
   BISAC: RELIGION / Christian Living / Prayer | RELIGION / Devotional
Classification: LCC BV210.3 .H377 2022 | DDC 248.3/2--dc23
LC record available at https://lccn.loc.gov/2021045520

Printed in the United States of America
22 23 24 25 26 27 28 29 / 8 7 6 5 4 3 2

To my daughters,
Kristen and Mary Leigh.

Because I wanted God's best
for you, I learned to pray.

contents

Part 4 | How Should I Pray?

Part 5 | What Should I Pray For?

Part 6 | Favorite Prayers from the Bible

preface

My life has changed three times (so far).

The first change happened when God cracked open my heart, showed me my sin, and covered it with His grace. I came to faith in Christ as an eighteen-year-old, Helen Reddy, "I Am Woman" kind of girl. Through the years, by God's good grace, He's been transforming me into a fifty-something-year-old "I Am *God's* Woman" kind of girl.

The second change occurred when I accepted the challenge to read my Bible through in a year. Before then, I'd known *of* God. After that, I began to *know* God. Really know Him. Like a besotted teenager, I discovered quality after quality that made me fall madly in love with Him. This love grows stronger every year.

The third change came about when I discovered prayer. Through Bible reading, I heard God speak to me. Through prayer, I learned that I could speak to God. It's an amazing thing to have a conversation with the God of the universe—heady and hope-filled. Joyous.

Soon my heart overflowed like a river at flood stage. I channeled the flow into my blog (LoriHatcher.com), then into teaching, article writing, and women's ministry speaking. I wrote a book, *Joy in the Journey: Encouragement for Homeschooling Moms* (That was an amazing God story). And another book, *Hungry for God . . . Starving for Time* (God story #2).

Now I'm working with Our Daily Bread Publishing to create the *Refresh* series. *Refresh Your Faith: Uncommon Devotions from Every Book of the Bible* is the first volume. You're holding *Refresh Your Prayers: Uncommon Devotions to Restore Power and Praise. Refresh Your Hope: 60 Unshakable Reasons Not to Lose Heart* will soon follow.

I write, speak, and live to point people to God and His Word. I want others to experience with me the power and presence of God available to us as believers in Jesus Christ. I'm so glad you've joined me on the journey.

Let the adventure begin!

introduction

Pastor and former US Senate chaplain Peter Marshall once said, "The whole field of prayer, and praying as laying hold on unlimited power, is unexplored, with the result that spiritual laws still lie undiscovered by the average believer." Another time he observed, "Sometimes, in our desperation, we hit upon the right way to pray, and things happen—our prayers are gloriously answered. But for the most part, our praying is very haphazard, and the results are often disappointing."[1]

For years, my prayer life was haphazard and disappointing. I felt like one of the squirrels that visited the bird feeder that hung from the eaves outside my dining room window.

Each fall I'd fill it with black oil sunflower seeds. The birds loved them, and I loved watching the birds. One day I noticed a squirrel sitting on the window ledge watching the chickadees, tufted titmice, and finches fill their bellies with the seeds I'd provided.

Mr. Squirrel knew those seeds were tasty, and he wanted some. He wanted to feast at the feeder like his feathered friends, but he couldn't reach it. He didn't know what the birds knew— he didn't know how to fly.

I watched him scamper back and forth on the window ledge trying to get to the feeder. He could see the shiny black seeds through the glass. I suspect he could smell their oily goodness. He certainly could hear the birds chattering about how wonderful the seeds tasted and how satisfying it felt to eat from the bounty I'd supplied.

In his first attempt to reach the feeder, the squirrel climbed up the side of the window frame. Then he dangled upside down from the top of it. He even jumped into the bushes, trying to use the branches as a ladder to reach the feeder. All with no success.

Finally, in a desperate attempt, he launched himself off the window ledge onto the top of the feeder. It spun like a merry-go-round. He held on for a few turns, then sailed off, landing in the grass with a plop.

For the rest of the day, he remained on the ground, scavenging for seeds the birds dropped.

My hungry squirrel's frustration and ultimate defeat resembled my prayer life more than I'd like to admit. I assumed prayer was a supernatural mystery that some believers understood but I didn't.

I read amazing promises in the Bible but saw few fulfilled in my life. I heard believers talk about dramatic answers to prayer, but I never experienced any. Some would even say God spoke to them during their prayer times. When I talked to God, I heard words coming from my mouth but nothing in response. I'd pray and pray and pray about things that weighed heavily on my heart, but nothing ever changed. What did others know that I didn't?

I felt like the squirrel who longed to eat from the feeder but didn't know how to reach it.

Thankfully, our heavenly Father invites us to eat at His table. Like the disciples who watched Jesus pray miracles into existence, we can come to Him and ask Him to be our teacher.

Luke 11:1 says, "One day Jesus was praying in a certain place.

When he finished, one of his disciples said to him, 'Lord, teach us to pray.'"

As we explore what the Bible teaches about prayer, we can be assured that Jesus, our gentle guide, will enlighten us. We'll draw closer to God, grow more confident and effective in our prayer lives, and experience the joy of feasting from God's bountiful table.

Part 1

What
Is
Prayer?

1

Prayer Was God's Idea

In the beginning God . . .

GENESIS 1:1

Do you remember the first text message you sent? I do. My family and I were camping. The kids splashed in the lake while I sat on the shore with Polly, our cocker spaniel, in my lap. We both jumped when my phone made a sound I'd never heard before.

I pulled it out of my pocket, flipped it open (remember those phones?), and—wonder of wonders!—read a message from my friend Alicia. I spent the next fifteen minutes figuring out how to respond. Trial, error, and a lot of backspacing taught me to push the number 5 twice for *K*, three times for *L*, and so on.

When I finally completed the ten-word message and sent it, I didn't realize the significance of the moment, but I do now. That (not so) brief exchange ushered in a new way of communicating.

The same thing happened to Adam and Eve. In the beginning of time, God walked and talked with Adam and Eve in the cool of the day. Communication between God and the people He created was as natural for them as breathing. Adam and Eve didn't have to read books, attend seminars, or figure out how to text on a flip phone. They just walked and talked with God.

Can you imagine the conversation?

"Lord," Adam might have said, "remember that crazy animal you brought to me? The one I named *platypus*? I saw it today, swimming in the pond. If you don't mind me asking, where'd you get the idea for such a creature, Lord?"

But then sin entered the world.

With Eve's first bite of the forbidden fruit, sin's poison spread, tainting the earth and the animals and people who lived on it. Although God had provided a temporary covering for their shame, sin continued to affect everything He had created—even mankind's ability to commune with their Creator.

Thankfully, God didn't stop talking with the people He had created. But something dramatic shifted. The world was no longer ideal.

While Adam and Eve didn't have flip phones tucked into the back pockets of their fig-leaf jeans, they had to learn a new way to communicate. They had to approach God differently. Face-to-face conversations weren't the norm anymore, but the channel of communication remained open.

Genesis 4:26 hints at this. "Seth also had a son, and he named him Enosh. At that time people began to call on the name of the LORD."

Adam was 130 years old when Seth was born. Seth was 105 when Enosh came along. That means Grandpa Adam was a spry 235 years old when people began to call on the name of the Lord again.

Perhaps Adam reminded them how God had initiated each conversation and invited them to communicate with Him. He may have recounted with longing how God would step out of heaven and walk with them in the cool of the evening. How they'd hear His footsteps in the garden and run to Him, eager to share what was on their hearts and how they'd spent their day. Surely Adam described how God responded to their words and pursued them, even when they went astray.

Much has happened since those early days of unhindered conversation. In God's mercy, we still possess the ability to communicate with our Creator. Some of the means and methods have changed, but like our spiritual forefathers, we were created to enjoy deep, intimate, dynamic conversations with God. He invites us to bring our needs, hopes, dreams, and fears to Him.

As we explore what the Bible teaches about prayer, we'll discover powerful principles to help us connect with God and experience the same kind of fellowship Adam and Eve enjoyed. Thankfully, it doesn't involve a flip phone with a clunky keyboard.

Genesis 1:1 reminds us that prayer, along with everything else, originated with God. It was His idea. It is part of the creation God deemed "very good."

"In the beginning God."

Uncommon Power

Although sin changed the way mankind talks with God, in a display of His amazing grace and love, He still wants us to communicate and have a relationship with Him.

Praise Prompt

Father, I'm so grateful that you didn't cut off communication forever on the day Adam and Eve sinned. Thank you for initiating prayer. I praise you for being a relational God who delights in communicating with His children. In Jesus's name I pray, amen.

Live It Out

Imagine what it would be like to walk and talk with God. Do you think it would be easier or harder to communicate with Him in person? What would you talk about? Today as you pray, picture that garden scene before sin corrupted communication. Talk to God freely about whatever's on your heart.

2

Prayer Is an Invitation to Partner with God

The LORD has done it this very day;
let us rejoice today and be glad.

PSALM 118:24

Jaqui is a master artist. In the time it takes most painters to select a brush and squeeze acrylic onto a palette, she can paint a landscape that would make Monet jealous.

She offered to paint a mural on the hallway leading to the children's wing of her church. "I'm going to do a big, bodacious Noah's ark scene," she announced during the painting class she taught each week. "Monkeys hanging from trees, giraffes on either side of the check-in desk, and droopy-eyed elephants at the end of the hall." She took a breath, then declared, "And I want you to help me. I'll come up with the plan and sketch the scene on the walls, then we'll have a painting party."

Noticing our skeptical faces, she added, "Don't worry. I'll coach you through it. It will be a masterpiece."

"But why include us?" one woman asked. "You could do it a whole lot faster on your own."

"I could," Jacqui said, "but it would be so much fun to do it together."

This conversation reminded me of one reason God invites us to pray—so we can experience the joy of working together.

Jaqui could have easily painted the mural. She didn't need her friends' help. But she wanted to do more than paint a hallway. She wanted to experience the joy of creating something beautiful together—and share that joy with her friends.

God, the master designer of our universe, doesn't need us to accomplish His work. He hung the world on nothing, laid the foundations of the earth, and established boundaries for the sea (Job 38). He causes nations to rise and fall and installs kings and presidents. He provides for those in need, heals the sick, and softens hard hearts.

He doesn't need our prayers to unlock His power, nor does He require our ideas to guide His hands. He invites us to pray because He wants to share the joy of doing His kingdom work.

I experienced a glimpse of this one night at church when Tabitha and Fernando asked our congregation to pray for their infant daughter's upcoming surgery. "The operation's scheduled for Friday," Fernando said. "The doctors say Bella will be in the hospital for at least ten days."

As I joined the others to pray for baby Bella, I said, "Lord, guide the surgeons' hands. Use their skill to heal her body. And, God, if it would bring you glory, please let her come home even sooner than ten days."

Late Friday night we learned the surgery had gone flawlessly. A week later the pastor announced, "Bella did so well they sent her home after only a week. Tabitha and Fernando thank you for your prayers."

I wept happy tears as I rejoiced in God's goodness on behalf of this precious family. And my heart swelled with joy to think that God would use my prayers as part of His work in their lives. I recognized, as the psalmist did in Psalm 118, "The LORD has done it this very day; let us rejoice and be glad."

As theologian and author C. S. Lewis wrote in his book *Miracles*, "The event [in question] certainly has been decided—in a sense it was decided 'before all worlds.' But one of the things taken into account in deciding it, and therefore one of the things that really cause it to happen, may be this very prayer that we are now offering."[2]

We don't always see the results of our prayers, but when we do, we experience the supernatural joy of partnering with God in His work.

Uncommon Power

Through prayer, God invites us into a holy cooperation—one that allows us to share the joy of accomplishing His will and His work in the world.

Praise Prompt

Heavenly Father, you are fully capable of running the universe without my help, yet you allow me the privilege and joy of being a part of your work in the world. Thank you for sharing the joy and excitement of what you're doing in people's lives every day. I love you so much. Amen.

Live It Out

Think back on some of the prayers God has answered in your life. Remember how your spirit leaped with joy at the pleasure of being part of God's work. Today, thank Him for allowing you to partner with Him through prayer. Ask Him to help you recognize the next opportunity He gives to be a part of the work He's doing in your world.

3

A Blood-Soaked Prayer

The LORD said, "What have you done?
Listen! Your brother's blood cries out
to me from the ground."

GENESIS 4:10

Have you ever had to ask someone for help when you knew you had treated them badly? I remember leaving my parents' house one day in a crash of slamming doors and angry words. Two miles down the road, I ran out of gas and had to call my dad to come rescue me. That was one of the hardest and most humiliating phone calls I've ever made.

The same can be true in how we relate with our heavenly Father.

If I'm at odds with God, willful in my disobedience, and rebellious in my attitude, I hesitate to come to Him for help, fellowship, or comfort. When my life, behavior, passions, and pursuits displease Him, I shy away. I avoid Him and turn my spiritual face when He beckons.

No doubt about it. Sin hinders prayer.

Cain experienced this, and Genesis 4 reveals his struggle. In this pivotal chapter in human history, we discover that the first prayer from earth to heaven didn't come from a person. It came from the ground.

"What have you done?" the Lord asked Cain after he murdered his brother. "Listen! Your brother's blood cries out to me from the ground" (v. 10).

The pool of Abel's blood declared Cain's barbaric deed. Every crimson drop proclaimed his sinful act and revealed the wicked heart that birthed it. It cried out for justice and punishment. Similarly, our transgressions stand as irrefutable evidence of our sinful state. Our guilt requires us to come to God for salvation and, later, for favor and help.

Yet God doesn't allow us to flounder hopelessly. He provides a means for sinful mankind to gain access to himself. He offered it to Cain, and He offers it to us—first for salvation and then for restoration.

In a conversation unrecorded in Scripture, God instructed Adam, Eve, and their two sons to bring offerings to Him. Abel complied, humbly offering God a firstborn animal from his flock. Cain came to God with a bag of grain and an arrogant heart.

When God refused to accept his offering, Cain became enraged.

At this point, God could have washed His holy hands of Cain, but He didn't. In love, He spoke tenderly to him.

"Why are you angry? Why is your face downcast? If you do what is right, will you not be accepted? But if you do not do what is right, sin is crouching at your door; it desires to have you, but you must rule over it" (vv. 6–7).

God's response demonstrated the patience He extends toward all of us, "not wanting anyone to perish, but everyone to come to repentance" (2 Peter 3:9).

While Abel's blood accused and condemned, Jesus's blood forgives and restores. Hebrews 12:23–24 states, "You have come to . . . Jesus the mediator of a new covenant, and to the sprinkled blood that speaks a better word than the blood of Abel." If we apply the blood of Jesus to our heart in faith, it provides unlimited access to the Father. Once salvation has removed the guilt of our sin, the blood of Christ continues to grant us access to our Father to confess our daily sins in prayer and restore our fellowship.

Come before me with a humble heart, God reasoned with Cain, *and I will bless you. I want to enjoy fellowship with you in a relationship that's unhindered by your willful independence and rebellion. But you must come to me on my terms.*

Sadly, Cain rejected God's grace-filled offer of salvation. He lived as a wanderer and a fugitive, fearful of men and banished from God's presence forever.

Our sin also stood between us and a holy God. But as He promised Adam and Eve in Genesis 3:15, He sent a sacrifice to pay the penalty for our sins—His Son, Jesus.

When Christ died on the cross, the perfect for the imperfect, the sinless for the sinful, He made a way for us to have a relationship with God. Jesus's blood, crying out from the cross, saved us from the penalty of sin that leads to eternal death. This same blood allows us to return again and again to our Father God for restoration whenever we sin against Him.

I felt embarrassed to ask my father to rescue me the day I ran out of gas, but we should never allow shame or regret to keep us from crying out to our heavenly Father. Because of Jesus's blood, we are forgiven. Nothing stands between our repentant prayers and the Father God who loves us.

Uncommon Power

We have access to God in prayer because of the blood of Jesus. His sacrifice means we can freely approach God.

Praise Prompt

Thank you, heavenly Father, for making a way for me to have a relationship with you. Because of this, I can come to you in prayer and find help in times of need. Thank you for not leaving me in my sin, estranged from you. I'm so grateful that you extend forgiveness and restoration every time I pray to you. Make my heart tender and submissive. Banish pride and arrogance from my life. In Jesus's name I pray, amen.

Live It Out

God extended the same offer of forgiveness and fellowship to Cain as He did to Abel. Abel accepted it. Cain rejected it. Are you an Abel or a Cain? How have you responded when God made you aware of your sin? As today's story shows, how we respond doesn't just affect our prayer life, it affects our eternity.

If you haven't yet trusted Christ as your Savior, what are you waiting for? Don't be a Cain. Accept God's offer of salvation today.

If you have a relationship with Christ, seek to confess sin as soon as you become aware of it. Don't allow sin to hinder your prayers and interfere with your fellowship with God.

4

Does God Speak to Me?

**When he, the Spirit of truth, comes, he will
guide you into all the truth. He will not speak
on his own; he will speak only what he hears,
and he will tell you what is yet to come.**

JOHN 16:13

If someone asked you to define prayer, what would you say? Most would agree that prayer is talking to God. But what about God talking to us?

The concept of a two-way conversation with God may sound like a trailer for an alternate-reality television show, but it's a very biblical concept. From the beginning of creation, God has spoken to His people. In the early days, before the Bible was complete, God spoke audibly to believers (Genesis 6:13). He also spoke through angelic messengers (Luke 1:11), Christophanies—preincarnate appearances of Christ (Genesis 18:22)—and prophets (Jeremiah 1:7). For a time, He spoke in the flesh through His Son, Jesus. But what about now? Does God still speak to people today?

He most certainly does. He speaks to us primarily through His Word, His messengers (pastors, teachers, and fellow believers), and the Holy Spirit's voice in our hearts.

As Jesus prepared to leave this world and return to His Father, He explained the Holy Spirit's part in our two-way dialogue: "When he, the Spirit of truth, comes, he will guide you into all the truth. He will not speak on his own; he will speak only what he hears, and he will tell you what is yet to come" (John 16:13).

If the Holy Spirit works in this way, why do we so often feel like prayer is a one-sided conversation? Missionary Frank Laubach expressed why most of us seldom hear God speak: "The trouble with nearly everybody who prays is that he says 'Amen' and runs away before God has a chance to reply. Listening to God is far more important than giving Him your ideas."[3]

But let's be honest. The fact that prayer is a two-way conversation makes it more complex, doesn't it? How do we know when God is speaking to us? And how can we be sure we're hearing His voice rather than our own thoughts or someone else's opinion? What can we do to experience a genuine two-way conversation grounded in truth?

We must learn to discern.

Here are five guidelines to help determine if what you hear is coming from the Lord:

1. What we hear must agree with Scripture. God never tells us to do something contrary to His Word. This is why we should read the Bible daily and become familiar with its truths. God intends it to be the standard to weigh other input.

2. God usually repeats an important message. We may read something that applies to our life in our morning quiet time, read something similar during a devotional reading, and hear a preacher mention the topic in a sermon. God's willingness to repeat himself is blessed confirmation if we think we're hearing from God but aren't quite sure. Journaling during our Bible reading and prayer time and taking notes during teaching and preaching times can help us recognize when God repeats himself.

3. An idea may come to us while we're praying. If it's something simple, like *Send Sally a note of encouragement. She's been struggling since Dan lost his job,* and isn't contrary to Scripture, I usually act upon it immediately. It's probably the Holy Spirit prompting me. If it involves a greater commitment, I test the thought by waiting to see if God reinforces it in other ways.

4. If an idea comes from the Lord, the desire usually grows stronger with time. I confess—sometimes I get some crazy ideas. Crazy or not, I write down the idea and begin to pray about it. As the days pass, I often find my enthusiasm and desire waning. Other times the desire grows, develops, and blossoms into a full-fledged calling. Usually, God confirms His direction in other ways and reinforces it with appropriate Scripture.

5. What I think God is telling me to do usually requires an element of risk and faith. Keep in mind that God seldom calls us to do something completely off the normal path of

our lives. Instead, His call is usually the next step, albeit sometimes a *big* step, on the path we're already walking on. As you seek confirmation from God, don't expect Him to answer every question and remove every barrier. If He did, we wouldn't have to exercise faith to obey Him, and faith is how we please God (Hebrews 11:6).

Our family has been involved in missions for years. We've financially supported missionaries, prayed for them, provided resources, and hosted them in our home. When my husband and I felt a desire stirring in our hearts to take a short-term missions trip with our family, we sensed it was from the Lord.

We prayed about it over a period of time, and the desire grew stronger. We knew mission work was biblical, so when missionary friends serving in Mexico mentioned they'd love to have a family come help with a short-term project, we knew God was calling us to go.

It seems a bit mysterious, but God intends for prayer to be a mutual conversation. With patience and practice, we can learn to recognize His voice. When we share our hearts with God and take time to listen to His Word, His messengers, and His still, small voice, we'll experience satisfying, intimate, and joy-filled conversations with Him.

Uncommon Power

Prayer is a two-way conversation. We talk to God, and He speaks to us. With time and practice, we can learn to recognize when He speaks and enjoy the delight of truly communicating with God.

Praise Prompt

Father, I stand amazed that you not only speak to us, but you guide and direct us to do your good purposes. I know following you will always require faith, yet you are willing and eager to share your heart with us. I'm amazed that you, the God of the universe, willingly enter into conversation with us. Remind me, every day, to sit in stillness, quieting my heart so I don't miss what you have to say to me. I love you, Father. Amen.

Live It Out

Use a journal during your prayer time to record meaningful Bible verses, prayers, and thoughts. List your prayers and how God answers them. Add any insight you receive from Bible study, sermons, or teaching times. From time to time, look back over your notes to see God's pattern of direction and guidance.

Part 2

The God
to Whom
We Pray

5

God Is Near

**When Jacob awoke from his sleep,
he thought, "Surely the LORD is in this
place, and I was not aware of it."**

GENESIS 28:16

Few people land in the hospital after making the bed, but my boss, Dr. Henry, did. One Saturday morning he leaned over to smooth out a wrinkle in the comforter, and something exploded like a firecracker in his lower back. He collapsed, face down on the bed. White-hot bursts of pain radiated from his waist to his foot and back again.

Responding to his cry for help, his wife called 911. An ambulance arrived and transported him to the local emergency room. There doctors determined he needed immediate surgery. Half-crazy with pain and frightened at the prospect of a major operation, his mind bounced from one scary thought to the next.

What will happen to my practice?

Who will take care of my family?

What if the damage is too great, and I'm paralyzed?

What if I never walk again?

He watched the ceiling tiles fly by until the doors to the operating room opened, and his bed stopped moving. A nurse anesthetist bent over him. A mask covered her face, but above it he could see blue eyes that perfectly matched the bonnet that covered her hair. Her eyes were kind. Reassuring.

Familiar.

"Sue?"

"Henry?"

"What are you doing here?" they exclaimed.

Dr. Henry knew Sue worked in the hospital, but in the panic and pain of the morning, he'd never considered she might be the nurse anesthetist assigned to his case.

Reflecting on the experience later, he said, "I knew I was going to be okay, because Sue was there."

You've probably experienced similar reassurances. Your mother cradled you in her arms after a nightmare. A friend walked beside you through a job loss, a marriage failure, or a loved one's death. A doctor promised, "We're in this together." The faithful, unwavering presence of a loved one or friend during a time of struggle is powerful.

For Christians, the greatest comfort of all is knowing God is with us. His ears are attentive to our cries. He is the unseen Presence, meeting our needs and orchestrating our circumstances. No matter what terror, crisis, or temptation touches our lives, God's nearness anchors our souls. We acknowledge that He is near every time we call out to Him in prayer.

Sometimes I forget God is with me and that I can cry out to Him. I'm not the only one. The patriarch Jacob, launching out into the unknown in search of a wife and a future, must have felt indescribably alone. In the wasteland, "a howling wilderness," he rested under the canopy of stars (Deuteronomy 32:10 NKJV). There God gave him a promise that startled him awake and changed him forever.

"I am with you and will watch over you wherever you go" (Genesis 28:15).

"Surely the LORD is in this place, and I was not aware of it," Jacob proclaimed (v. 16). God is here, and He is with me wherever I go.

David the psalmist experienced a similar revelation. Pondering how God had known him before he was born and promised to be with him to his dying breath and beyond, he penned Psalm 139, one of the most beloved and confident psalms of God's enduring presence.

"Where can I go from your Spirit? Where can I flee from your presence? If I go up to the heavens, you are there; if I make my bed in the depths, you are there. If I rise on the wings of the dawn, if I settle on the far side of the sea, even there your hand will guide me, your right hand will hold me fast" (vv 7–10).

Isaiah painted a beautiful picture of God's presence when he wrote, "For this is what the high and exalted One says—he who lives forever, whose name is holy: 'I live in a high and holy place, but also with the one who is contrite and lowly in spirit'" (Isaiah 57:15).

Theologians call the concept of God's omnipresence "divine immanence." I call it powerful comfort. The God of Jacob, David, and Isaiah is our God too. He hears our cries and is nearer than our breath, our heartbeat, and our trials.

Uncommon Power

Wherever we are and whatever we go through, we can pray knowing that God is the unseen Presence who is right here with us.

Praise Prompt

I praise you, Father, for being my steadfast hope when all around me gives way. Though the mountains be removed and crash into the sea, your presence will remain forever. Thank you for your many promises never to leave me nor forsake me. Thank you for hearing my prayers. I'm so grateful I can say with confidence, "The Lord is my helper; I will not be afraid" (Hebrews 13:6).

Live It Out

What current situation causes you to feel anxious or afraid? What concern steals the sleep from your nights and the joy from your days? Picture what it would look like if, every step of the way, you could see God walking by your side. Would this change the way you talked (prayed) to Him? Would it change the way you felt and responded? Today and every day, keep this thought in the forefront of your mind: God is here.

6

We Pray to a Person

Moses said to God, "Suppose I go to the
Israelites and say to them, 'The God of
your fathers has sent me to you,' and they
ask me, 'What is his name?' Then what
shall I tell them?" God said to Moses,
"I AM WHO I AM."

EXODUS 3:13–14

In my ten years as the editor of *Reach Out, Columbia* magazine, I interviewed some well-known and influential people: international ministry leader Anne Graham Lotz; Dove Award–winners Steven Curtis Chapman, Fernando Ortega, and Laura Story; book authors Sally Lloyd-Jones, Kevin Leman, and Gary Chapman; and comedian Tim Hawkins.

As I prepared to talk with one of these important men or women, I'd sometimes feel nervous. My heart would race, and my palms would sweat. What if I forgot a question or said something dumb?

Years of experience, however, taught me a valuable truth. No matter how many awards someone's won or how many countries they've preached the gospel in, regardless of the number of sold-out concerts they've performed or how highly esteemed they are, they're still just people.

I learned to look beyond their celebrity status and interact with them as human beings. I asked Anne Graham Lotz about her aging father, Billy. I asked Steven Curtis Chapman about his kids. I discovered Gary Chapman likes oatmeal cookies, and Tim Hawkins sometimes embarrasses his children. Approaching them as people calmed my fears and helped me get to know them.

This same approach helps me come to God in prayer.

After all, He's more powerful than the president, more intelligent than the smartest human being, and able to summon earthquakes, floods, and plagues with a flick of His finger. He's so incredibly holy that angels praise His name night and day in the throne room of heaven. He is the Great I AM who turned water to blood, summoned darkness to cover the land, and parted the Red Sea. It's easy to be intimidated and see Him as unapproachable and frightening.

Me have a conversation with the God of the universe? Pull up a chair and share my thoughts, feelings, and fears? Uh, no. I don't think so.

Yet we can if we remember God is a Person. He's not a human-being person, but a holy God Person with a mind, emotions, and will. He's an all-knowing and awe-inspiring Person but a Person nonetheless. He has thoughts, feelings, and ideas. He loves and laughs, grieves and cries. He brags on His children (Job 1:8; Genesis 26:5) and takes pride in His work. He's creative, expressive, and funny. If you doubt this, look at an ostrich or a penguin.

Yes, He's omniscient, omnipresent, and self-existing, but He's also the intimate Father who created us—right down to the swirl of our fingerprints and the shape of our ears. He's our Bridegroom and Shepherd, a friend of sinners and the lover of our souls.

The Great I AM is a Person who loves us and invites us to talk with Him every day. The next time you approach Him in prayer, think on this and watch how it transforms your interactions with God.

Uncommon Power

God is not only the Great I AM who can work miracles; He's also a Person I can laugh and cry with in prayer and talk to about even the smallest details of my day.

Praise Prompt

Father, you are worthy of praise and deserving of honor. You need nothing, yet you desire a relationship with me. You invite me to talk with you. To pour out my heart and share my thoughts. To speak with you, as Moses did, as a person talks to his friend. Thank you for inviting me to come before you today.

Live It Out

Today, as you approach God in prayer, picture Him seated on His throne, high and lifted up. Then imagine Him as your good Father and your dearest friend. Each viewpoint is true. Each should impact how you relate to Him. Praise Him as the King of Kings and Lord of Lords, then talk to Him as your Father and your Friend.

7

God Doesn't Have a Phone Tree

Before they call I will answer; while they are still speaking I will hear.

ISAIAH 65:24

In the age of cell phones, there's no such thing as a busy signal. If someone doesn't want to take your call, they silence it or decline it and send it to voice mail.

A friend shared a recent communication frustration. "I was trying to get information from a doctor's office. I climbed every branch of the phone tree and left three voice mails—no response. I called in the morning, at lunchtime, and at midafternoon. Finally, I drove down to the office and camped out in the waiting room until I could speak to a person who could help me. Sheesh! Three days of my life I can never get back again."

I'm thankful God doesn't ignore our attempts to reach Him. Isaiah 65:24 tells us He does the exact opposite. "Before they call I will answer; while they are still speaking I will hear." Unlike people who dodge our calls, don't listen to our messages, and refuse to respond to our requests, God answers us *before we call* and *while we are still speaking.*

We don't have to climb a ten-limb phone tree when we need help. Instead, we can cry out to God and hear His kind voice respond, "How may I help you?"

Peter supplies the New Testament version of Isaiah 65:24 in 1 Peter 3:12: "For the eyes of the Lord are on the righteous and his ears are attentive to their prayer."

His ears are attentive to their prayer—oh, what marvelous words. What a comforting thought. Unlike us, God isn't selfish and lazy in His hearing. He is attentive and caring.

I don't know how many times as a child I stuffed my fingers in my ears to muffle the sound of my family's voices. Maybe my sisters annoyed me with their requests or pestered me with their nonstop chatter. Perhaps Mom called me to do a chore I didn't want to do or Dad reminded me to do my homework.

When I didn't want to hear what they had to say or respond to their words, I pretended not to hear them. Or cranked up the stereo to drown out their voices. Sometimes I deliberately blocked out the sound of their requests.

God isn't like this. He not only hears; He responds—sometimes even before the words leave our mouths.

Prayer is talking to an attentive God about what matters most to us.

Uncommon Power

God is so attentive to our prayers that He answers us before we even finish praying.

Praise Prompt

Oh, Father, who are we to deserve an audience with you? You could easily limit your attention to more important people, but you don't. Your ears hear even our faintest prayer. Your infinite power sits poised to work on our behalf. Your mercy is great, and your love is abundant. Thank you for being a God who delights in the prayers of His children and rewards our desire to reach out to you in faith. In the strong name of Jesus I pray, amen.

Live It Out

How can the truth of today's Scriptures impact your prayer life? If you truly believed God heard and responded to every prayer you prayed, would you pray more confidently? More eagerly? When you don't see immediate results, could you rest in the knowledge that because God is, indeed, at work, His answer will come? Today, picture God's eyes upon you. Visualize His ears attentive to your prayers. Imagine Him springing into action as the first whisper leaves your lips. This isn't just wishful thinking. It's truth you can live by.

8

Resting in God's Sovereignty

**"For my thoughts are not your thoughts,
neither are your ways my ways," declares
the LORD. "As the heavens are higher than
the earth, so are my ways higher than your
ways and my thoughts than your thoughts."**

ISAIAH 55:8-9

One morning I received a heartbreaking comment from a reader in response to one of my blog posts on prayer.

"Can't bring back all the dead friends/family members I prayed for God to save," she wrote. "Praying to preserve the few family I had left didn't work either (down to one). Praying for healing from a health issue that has gone on for TWO YEARS and made my life miserable. Praying for this, praying for that, my heart gets hard when I get down on my knees. Just feels stupid. I can't make myself believe."[4]

As I bowed my head in prayer, I didn't pray for her only. I prayed for all the weary warriors wondering if their prayers were accomplishing anything and whether God really cares.

And if He does, why would He answer our petitions with what appears to be the exact opposite of what we prayed for? Is it because our faith isn't strong enough? Maybe prayer doesn't work. Or perhaps God isn't good.

The prophet Habakkuk didn't comment on blog posts, but he wasn't afraid to ask God questions. His example helps us puzzle through the mysteries of "bad" answers to "good" prayers.

"How long, LORD, must I call for help, but you do not listen?" he wrote. "Or cry out to you, 'Violence!' but you do not save? Why do you make me look at injustice? Why do you tolerate wrongdoing? Destruction and violence are before me; there is strife, and conflict abounds" (Habakkuk 1:2–3).

Habakkuk was a godly, tenderhearted man grieving for his country. Everywhere he turned he saw violence, perversion, and a wanton disdain for God and His ways. His countrymen had turned their backs on all that was good and right, and danced merrily along a path leading straight to destruction. In vain he warned the people of Judah, pleading for them to forsake evil and turn back to God. He begged God to soften their hearts and draw them back to himself. He prayed for God's mercy to lead His people to repentance.

God responded to Habakkuk's prayers with words that took his breath away.

"I am raising up the Babylonians, that ruthless and impetuous people, who sweep across the whole earth to seize dwellings not their own. They are a feared and dreaded people; they are a law to themselves and promote their own honor" (Habakkuk 1:6–7).

Habakkuk prayed for God's mercy to lead his countrymen to repentance. Instead, God sent a cruel and godless army to conquer the nation and carry them off to Babylon.

What kind of God does this?

What kind of God hears an earnest prayer for healing and allows death to take our loved one? Or a desperate prayer for reconciliation and allows our marriage to end in divorce? Or a trusting prayer for provision and allows poverty instead? What kind of God allows unemployment, illness, and heartbreak when He could speak a word and make everything right again?

Only a God of love.

A God of love? Really?

These are hard words to accept, and they introduce an even harder concept. But if we are to be men and women of faith, we must trust and believe what the Bible says about God:

God is love (Romans 5:8) and loving (1 John 4:10).

God is wise (Proverbs 3:19).

God is merciful (Psalm 145:9 NKJV).

God is kind (Lamentations 3:33).

God is just (Luke 18:7).

God is all-powerful (Jeremiah 32:17) and all-knowing (1 John 3:20).

When we, as Habakkuk did, receive an answer to prayer that appears to be the opposite of what we asked for, we must trust that there are bigger things happening than what we see unfolding in front of us.

This is the moment when faith stares fear in the face—and faith must win. "Without faith," Hebrews 11:6 says, "it is impossible to please God, because anyone who comes to him must believe that he exists and that he rewards those who earnestly seek him." And when we seek Him, really seek Him, He blesses us with the greatest reward of all—the presence and power of Jesus Christ.

We must stake our lives on the truth that God is a good God with a good plan that will ultimately surpass anything we could ever hope for or imagine (Ephesians 3:20). Through the events of our lives and the answers to our prayers, God will glorify himself and work for our ultimate good (Romans 8:28). He will remain true to His nature and accomplish His divine purposes for us and in us.

But sometimes good looks bad. A cruel army invades Judah and carries off God's chosen people. An innocent caretaker gets accused of rape and spends years in jail (Genesis 39). A God-fearing man prays in his home and gets sentenced to the lions' den (Daniel 6).

The sinless Son of God suffers and dies on a cruel Roman cross (1 Peter 2:24).

"'For my thoughts are not your thoughts, neither are your ways my ways,' declares the LORD. 'As the heavens are higher than the earth, so are my ways higher than your ways and my thoughts than your thoughts'" (Isaiah 55:8–9).

When we receive answers to prayer that fly in the face of all that seems good and right, we have a choice: to rage or to rest. We can rage against the circumstances that threaten us, or we can rest in the strong arms of God's wisdom and love.

Job made his choice: "Though he slay me, yet will I hope in him" (Job 13:15).

God used the cruel army that invaded Judah and carried off God's chosen people to bring about a national revival. God used the innocent caretaker jailed for rape to save millions of people from starvation. God used the praying man thrown into a lions' den to testify before kings and record a vision of the end times.

And God used His sinless, holy Son, who suffered and died on a cruel Roman cross, to secure eternal life for all who will believe.

We don't know if Habakkuk lived to see the good things God accomplished through the tragedy of the Babylonian invasion, but we know he had the opportunity to stare fear in the face and choose faith.

"I heard and my heart pounded, my lips quivered at the sound; decay crept into my bones, and my legs trembled. Yet I will wait patiently for the day of calamity to come on the nation invading us. Though the fig tree does not bud and there are no grapes on the vines, though the olive crop fails and the fields produce no food, though there are no sheep in the pen and no cattle in the stalls, yet I will rejoice in the LORD, I will be joyful in God my Savior" (Habakkuk 3:16–19).

Uncommon Power

Faith in God's good nature allows us to pray and rest in quiet trust.

Praise Prompt

Father, thank you that when I don't understand what you're doing, I can rest in what I know about you. When you send answers to my prayers that don't look at all like what I asked for, help me remember that although your ways are not my ways, they are good. Grow my faith. Increase my trust. Fill me with joy so others will see and believe. In the precious name of Jesus I ask, amen.

Live It Out

How would your prayer life be different if you clung to the truth that God is sovereignly working for your good and His glory? Would you respond differently to the challenging situations in your life? Pray in faith, wait in trust, and rest in the fact that God is good.

Part 3

Why Pray?

9

Responding to God's Prompting

**No one can come to me unless the Father
who sent me draws them.**

JOHN 6:44

Prayer is a lonely business. When the answers are long in coming, I sometimes wonder if my prayers bother God. Does He look through the peephole of heaven and sigh as I do when I see the door-to-door salesperson headed down my sidewalk? *Oh no. Here she comes again.*

Jesus told us exactly how God feels in John 6:44 when He said, "No one can come to me unless the Father who sent me draws them." Although the passage primarily describes how God draws people to salvation, the principle also applies to our prayers.

We pray because God draws us.

Have you ever wondered why you wake up in the middle of the night thinking about that wayward child? God is drawing you to pray. Why you feel a tug in your heart to intercede for a missionary, ask God to meet someone's need, or repeat a request you've prayed about for years? God is calling you to pray. Why that "random" memory of someone you haven't seen in decades comes to mind? God is prompting you to intercede for them.

For years I assumed the desire to pray originated in me. I'd see a need and pray about it. (Usually after I'd unsuccessfully tried to solve the problem on my own.)

John 6:44 turned my perspective on prayer upside down. It showed me people don't naturally seek God—for salvation or for help. We try to handle it ourselves. We harness our energy, skill, and stamina, and attempt to make it happen. We manipulate, persuade, cajole, and guilt. We bargain. We cry. We stomp.

When we've exhausted ourselves and collapsed in futility, God draws us to himself in prayer. Little by little, we learn to recognize the prompts of the Holy Spirit and respond to these nudges by praying.

When you became aware of a need and felt moved to pray, God drew you. He brought the person across your path, helped you recognize their need, and gave you the faith to pray. He did this because He's already working in that situation.

It's not a coincidence you pray for your prodigal five times a day. It's evidence God is working in your loved one's life. It's not random that you're moved to pray for a sick baby in the hospital or a coworker struggling with an addiction. God is working in those situations too. And that prayer request you've brought to God a thousand times? It is proof that God is orchestrating a thousand circumstances to accomplish His good and perfect will.

He doesn't need our prayers to accomplish His work, but He uses them as a conduit for His power. In love and fellowship, He invites us to be part of what He's already doing.

Jesus reminded His disciples, "My Father is always at his work to this very day" (John 5:17).

I take great comfort in knowing that every time God brings a need to my attention and stirs my heart to pray, it's because He's already at work.

I'd be a terrible pray-er if it wasn't for God inspiring, prompting, and directing. The more I learn to recognize His nudges and respond, the more God allows me to be part of His work in the world.

Uncommon Power

God prompts us to pray because He's already working in the situation.

Praise Prompt

Oh, Father, you fill my heart with hope as I realize that every time I feel the urge to pray, you are behind it. My inclinations to pray demonstrate you're already at work in the situation. This knowledge helps me persevere in prayer, even when I see no signs of change. Thank you, Father, for always working in our world and for inviting me to be a part of what you're doing. May your steadfast purposes prevail. In the powerful name of Jesus I pray, amen.

Live It Out

How much more hope-filled and empowered might you feel if you viewed every prayer prompt as evidence God is already at work in that situation? Is there something in your life about which you've felt tempted to despair or lose hope? Instead of doubting, thank God for moving you to pray. Thank Him for working in that situation to accomplish His good and perfect will. Express your gratitude for allowing you to be a part of the journey. Acknowledge your trust in Him and pray on.

10

Growing in Relationship with God

Now this is eternal life: that they know
you, the only true God, and
Jesus Christ, whom you have sent.

JOHN 17:3

If you ask people to describe God, among a hundred other adjectives, they might use the words *omniscient*, *omnipotent*, and *sovereign*.

Omniscient means God knows everything.

Omnipotent means He's all-powerful.

Sovereign means He controls everything.

While theologically accurate, these words can cause us to stumble in our prayer lives. If God is all-knowing, all-powerful, and all-controlling, why should we pray? Isn't God going to do what He wants to do regardless of our prayers?

This question arises from a wrong understanding of why we pray. We don't pray to convince God to do something He doesn't want to do, like a kid trying to persuade his mom to give him a cookie when she'd prefer not to.

We don't pray to give God an idea or information He doesn't already have, either, like little Jimmy telling Mom the cookies are in the cupboard, and he'd really like one. Nor do we pray to hold God to a promise, like Jimmy reminding Mom she promised him a cookie yesterday, so she'd better make good on her word.

God invites us to pray for many reasons, but the primary reason is to cultivate a relationship with us.

We become His children when we accept His offer of salvation and place our faith in Christ, but like a baby, we don't automatically trust Him. It takes time to learn His nature.

When our earthly parents respond to our cries, we discover they are faithful. We learn they're able to meet our needs when they feed us, change our diapers, and protect us from danger. When we ask them questions and listen to their answers, we realize they are wise. As we mature, we learn what makes them happy and what makes them sad.

God reveals His nature to us through prayer. The ebb and flow of conversation, thoughts, ideas, and emotions help us get to know Him.

In spiritual infancy, need prompts most of our prayers. "God, I need help with this test. Please help me remember what I've studied." "God, my mom's sick. Help her feel better." "God, I need money to go to college. Please provide for me." As He hears our prayers and meets our needs, we learn He is trustworthy.

One year, as I read through my Bible during my prayer time, I listed His character qualities. Patient, kind, merciful, forgiving, wise, creative, just, generous, strong, unchanging, dependable, all-powerful, and all-knowing. As my list grew, my love for Him grew.

As I prayed and God replied through His Word, the Bible, I learned what pleased Him and what made Him angry, what brought Him joy and what hurt His heart. Because I loved Him, I yearned to please Him. This motivated me to obey His commands and follow His instructions (John 14:15). Like my physical parents, my heavenly Father guided me on good paths.

In response to my prayers, the still, small voice of God's Spirit would sometimes speak to me using the verses I'd stored in my heart. During times of crisis, God would whisper Psalm 56:3, "Whenever I am afraid, I will trust in You" (NKJV). When I felt sad, I sensed God's arms around me as He brought Psalm 34:18 to mind, "The LORD is close to the brokenhearted."

Although I began my prayer journey with a one-sided monologue of needs, I soon discovered that one of the sweetest reasons God calls us to pray is so we can grow in our relationship with Him. What a privilege. What a gift.

Uncommon Power

God invites us to pray because He desires for us to be in a close, connected relationship with Him.

Praise Prompt

Precious Lord, perfect Father, you have loved me from the beginning and invited me to experience the pleasure of a relationship with you. Prayer helps me know your heart, feel your love, work alongside you, and share your joy and sorrow. Help me to never take our relationship for granted, but nurture and cultivate it every day. In the sweet and tender name of Jesus I pray, amen.

Live It Out

Consider your prayer life. Do you primarily seek God for the gifts He provides? Have you ever considered that prayer might be an invitation from God to know Him better and experience a closer relationship with Him? Beginning today, ask God to reveal himself to you. Look for Him on the pages of Scripture and in the world around you. Note what you see, and respond in love and gratitude.

11

Sharing God's Heart

**I will remove from you your heart of stone
and give you a heart of flesh.**

EZEKIEL 36:26

I used to think the purpose of prayer was to change God's mind—to persuade Him to do what I wanted Him to do. I assumed if I had to pray about something, it was because God wasn't doing what needed to be done.

Oh, how wrong I was.

When we pray, something transformative happens. As we share our hearts with God and listen for Him to respond to us through His Word and the Holy Spirit, God opens the channel between our minds and His. When we confess our sin, we remove the debris that blocks the unhindered flow of thought, and we're better able to understand Him and His ways. Oswald Chambers wrote in *Christian Disciplines*, "Prayer is . . . the means whereby we assimilate more and more of His mind."[5]

Instead of eavesdropping on God's thinking, the Holy Spirit within us helps bring our thinking in line with God's. This may seem improbable, but 1 Corinthians 2:16 affirms it. If we are God's children, "we have the mind of Christ."

But we don't just have His mind; we have His heart. "I will give you a new heart and put a new spirit in you," God said through the prophet Ezekiel. "I will remove from you your heart of stone and give you a heart of flesh" (Ezekiel 36:26). The more we get to know God, the more He transforms our hearts, thoughts, and desires.

Jennifer Kennedy Dean, in *Live a Praying Life*, describes the process this way: "It is through the ongoing and increasingly intimate communion with Him that our participation in the divine nature becomes solid and real. Through prayer, He is reproducing His heart in us."[6]

Most miraculous of all, as we become conformed to the image of God's Son, our prayers become more powerful, because we pray according to His will and desires. We pray the prayers God is pleased to answer. We ask for what He wants to give us.

"This is the confidence we have in approaching God: that if we ask anything according to his will, he hears us. And if we know that he hears us—whatever we ask—we know that we have what we asked of him" (1 John 5:14–15).

How do we know what His will is? We get to know His mind and heart through prayer and God's Word. Only Christians have the privilege of interacting with the God who not only created us but wants a relationship with us.

As we seek God in prayer, the Holy Spirit, who knows God's mind, will be our teacher. He'll shape and direct our prayers. He'll transform them into petitions God delights to answer because they reflect His will.

In my early days of prayer, I approached God to change His mind. Now I come to Him so He can change mine.

Uncommon Power

Prayer transforms us and makes our hearts and minds more like God's.

Praise Prompt

Heavenly Father, thank you for being a God who delights to share your thoughts, desires, and plans with us. What an amazing concept—that we can speak with the God of the universe, and you speak back. Thank you for inviting us into your heart and mind and making us more and more like yourself.

Live It Out

As you pray and read your Bible today, invite God to transform your heart and mind and make it more like His. Ask Him to help you love what He loves and hate what He hates. As you move through your day, filter your thoughts through the truth of God's Word and adjust accordingly.

12

Learning to Trust

He said to his disciples, "Why are you so afraid? Do you still have no faith?"

MARK 4:40

Our dog Winston was the biggest scaredy cat in the canine world. We credit his timidity to his time in "the big house." The runt of the litter, seven-week-old Winston was malnourished and mangy when someone dropped him off at the animal shelter.

Thankfully the animal control officer was married to Grace, the president of the animal rescue league. He told her about the tiny, freckle-faced puppy, and she saw potential in him. Eying his patchy fur and protruding ribs, she announced, "I can cure his mange and fatten him up. He'll make someone a great pet."

Until his mange cured, Grace kept Winston isolated. By the time we adopted him, he'd spent a large portion of his life alone. We weren't surprised to discover he had trust issues.

Imagine what it would be like to go from an isolated crate in the corner of a room to a big wide world bustling with sights, sounds, and smells. Falling leaves sent him running for cover. Sudden noises caused him to hide under the nearest piece of furniture. One day we were playing in an open field when a plastic grocery bag blew his way. He bolted like Sasquatch was chasing him.

Winston reminds me of myself in the early days of my faith. God didn't rescue me from the big house, but He did rescue me from a dark and hopeless future. He cured my sin sickness and promised to take care of me all the days of my life.

But I had trust issues. At the first rustle of change or clatter of trouble, I ran for cover. Like the disciples in the storm on the Sea of Galilee, I cried out, "Teacher, don't you care about me?"

I was convinced—God was sleeping, and I was going to drown.

I had to extend lots of love and patience to persuade Winston to trust me. When scary things frightened him, I called his name, dropped to my knees, and opened my arms wide.

"Come, Winston," I said. "Come to me. I'll protect you."

Before long he learned to run *to* me instead of away from me. One day I walked him on a busy street to condition him not to fear traffic noises. In the distance a fire truck roared our way. Seeing the threat, I dropped to my knees, wrapped my arms around him, and covered him with my body until the truck howled past.

"Don't be afraid," I whispered into his trembling ear. "I've got you."

God did the same for me. As I prayed and He answered, I learned to run to Him whenever anything frightening entered my world. When I brought financial needs, sickness, and relationship troubles to Him in prayer, I saw Him respond. When the leaves of uncertainty rustled, I shared my fears with Him. When unemployment, a wayward child, or a troubling situation roared into my life, I sought protection in His mighty arms and found comfort and help. As He answered my prayers and responded to my needs, my trust grew.

"Don't be afraid," God whispered to my trembling heart. "I've got you."

Sometimes I wish I didn't have to pray about everything. Wouldn't it be wonderful if God met my needs; kept me free from sickness, pain, and sorrow; and intercepted every problem before it touched my life?

If He did, though, I'd never learn to trust Him. My faith would be as malnourished as Winston when Grace rescued him. I'd take every good gift for granted and never recognize that it came from the generous hand of my heavenly Father.

In heaven, nothing will make me afraid, and my faith will become sight. Until then, my fear drives me to pray, and God's answers grow my faith.

As Winston learned to trust me, our relationship grew sweeter. No longer plagued by fear and distrust, he could freely enjoy the life we shared.

As I've learned to trust God, our relationship has grown sweeter too. I've learned He's not asleep on the job. He's aware of all my needs and is fully able to meet them. This knowledge frees me to face life with confidence.

Jesus asked His disciples two questions in the middle of the storm. He asks us the same: "Why are you so afraid?" and "Do you still have no faith?" Because faith pleases God, I'm learning to embrace every need that sends me running into His arms. No matter what threatens, I find them always open.

Uncommon Power

God calls me to pray so I can learn to trust Him.

Praise Prompt

Father, thank you for patiently teaching me to love and trust you. I praise you for being trustworthy, faithful, and good. Grow my faith, Lord. When trials and trouble enter my life, help me run to you first. In the strong name of Jesus I ask, amen.

Live It Out

List all the ways God has provided for you in the last week. In the last month. In the last year. List everything from the air in your lungs, to the clothes on your back, to the roof over your head. Think also of the nonmaterial gifts. Has God been faithful? Remember this the next time you feel afraid. Run to Him and grow in faith and trust.

13

Fellowshipping with the Trinity

Very early in the morning, while it was still dark, Jesus got up, left the house and went off to a solitary place, where he prayed.

MARK 1:35

One day I heard a voice coming from my walk-in closet.

This didn't surprise me. My grandchildren love my closet. Some days they pretend they're cougars and my closet is their den. Other times they're princesses and my closet is their royal dressing room. Once my closet was a dungeon where they locked up their baby brother and turned out the light.

But this day, all four kids were accounted for except one—four-year-old Caroline. As I neared the closet, I heard her talking. I crept to the doorway and paused, straining my ears to hear her tiny voice. The sweet conversation Caroline was having with herself made me smile.

Don't you wish you could have sneaked up on Jesus in His prayer closet? Wouldn't you love to hear what He and His Father talked about?

We know Jesus was fully God as He walked the earth, but He was also fully man. In order to experience the full measure of life as a human being, Christ voluntarily set aside the use of His deity. Every day He sought God for insight, direction, wisdom, and provision.

Scripture records times when Jesus sought God's guidance. He prayed all night before He chose his disciples (Luke 6:12). He prayed for power to do the tasks God had called Him to do (Matthew 26:42). He prayed for little children (19:13), and He prayed for His friends (John 17:9).

But there were other times—when Jesus went off by himself to a solitary place to pray—that we know nothing about. No one listened outside the door of His closet, straining to hear His voice and taking notes.

What did He pray for? Why did He pray? He had no sin to confess or inadequacies to make up for. He didn't question His calling or His mission, and He didn't wonder where His next meal was coming from. God had always supplied His needs.

I believe He prayed for the sweetest reason of all—because He desired fellowship with His Father. As the second member of the Trinity, Jesus always had unlimited access to the Father and to the Holy Spirit, but during His time on earth, He communicated with God as we do—through prayer.

Today, we can enjoy the same type of free-flowing conversation Jesus had. As Christians, the Spirit of God lives within us. He connects us with God's heart, speaks to us through God's Word, and guides us into all truth.

When we make time, as Jesus did, to get alone with the Father, we can sense God's presence. Sitting quietly before Him with our Bibles open prepares us to learn from the Holy Spirit as He brings the Scriptures to light. A passage becomes more than just words on a page. It becomes an intimate conversation between friends.

With no agenda, we're free to enjoy God for who He is, not just for what we can get from Him. We can snuggle into the comfort of His companionship and find safety in His strong presence. Like a small child, we can come to Him—just as we are—and find His arms open and His lap inviting. Who else knows all about us yet welcomes us with such tenderness and grace?

Prayer can become a place to share with God the yearnings and desires of our hearts. He'll listen, allowing us to voice our hopes, dreams, and fears. He affirms, directs, and redirects. With infinite kindness and unlimited grace, He draws us to His heart.

That day in the closet, I heard Caroline talking to herself. If I were to eavesdrop on Jesus, I'd hear Him talking to himself too. God the Son talking with God the Father and God the Holy Spirit, the divine three-in-one, enjoying their relationship. Sharing their hearts. Delighting in each other's presence.

And the greatest wonder of all? God—Father, Son, and Holy Spirit—invites us to join Him in the closet of prayer.

"I have called you friends," Jesus told His disciples, "for everything that I learned from my Father I have made known to you" (John 15:15).

What are you waiting for? Come on in.

Uncommon Power

God the Father, Son, and Holy Spirit calls us to fellowship in prayer.

Praise Prompt

God, I marvel at the way you invite me into fellowship and conversation with you every day. You call me your friend! What a privilege. May I always be eager to spend time with you in Bible reading and prayer. In Jesus's name I pray, amen.

Live It Out

Today when you pray, set aside your lists and focus on God. Praise Him for His attributes. Thank Him for His work in your life. Reflect on His majesty. Enjoy His presence. Remember His history of faithfulness through the ages. Listen to Him speak to you through the voice of the Holy Spirit and His Word. Enter into the fellowship already taking place between the Father, Son, and Holy Spirit.

14

Finding God

**Then you will call on me and come and pray to
me, and I will listen to you. You will seek me and
find me when you seek me with all your heart.**

JEREMIAH 29:12-13

There's nothing like a prodigal to drive you to your knees.

Whether your prodigal is a wayward child, a straying spouse, or a lost loved one, battling for someone's soul will turn a casual pray-er into a seasoned warrior.

Although I've always prayed for my family's health, safety, and spiritual welfare, I entered a new season of intercession when a family member waded into dark and dangerous waters. If God didn't intervene, I feared my loved one would be swept away in a riptide of unbelief, rebellion, and poor choices.

Fear and desperation drew me to my prayer closet every morning. I wept. I grieved. I lamented. I vacillated between soaring hope and deep despair. I knew God could bring my loved one into a relationship with himself, but I didn't know if He would.

As the weeks turned into months, and the months turned into years, I poured out my heart to God, and He met me there.

When I first prayed, all I could do was cry. My hurt, disappointment, and fear overwhelmed me, paralyzing me with its intensity. After I'd talk (cry) to God, I'd open His Word, searching for a measure of hope or comfort. Like a drowning person grasping for anything that floats, I cobbled together a life raft out of the verses I read.

> He will never leave you nor forsake you. (Deuteronomy 31:8)

> The Lord . . . is patient with you, not wanting anyone to perish, but everyone to come to repentance. (2 Peter 3:9)

> This is what the Lord says: "Restrain your voice from weeping, and your eyes from tears, for your work will be rewarded," declares the Lord. "They will return from the land of the enemy." (Jeremiah 31:16)

As I prayed, a strange thing happened. Nothing changed with my loved one's circumstances, yet I grew more hopeful. More peaceful. More joy-filled.

God became dear to me in ways I'd never experienced. He became a trusted friend who listened, empathized, and grieved with me. Everywhere I looked, I saw evidence of His love and care.

He'd whisper a promise on the pages of Scripture or breathe a word of hope through song lyrics. He sent believing friends to lift my weary arms and pray for me. The still, small voice of the Holy Spirit banished Satan's lies from my mind and brought much-needed perspective.

Although I'd reached the point where I felt as though everything precious had been stripped away, I discovered something even more valuable—God's presence in the midst of my trial. Nineteenth-century preacher Charles H. Spurgeon articulated this beautifully when he said, "You will never know the fullness of Christ until you know the emptiness of everything else but Christ."[7]

During my trial, when I felt as though God was all I had, I realized God was all I needed.

"God," I prayed one morning, "you've been so faithful to me. You surround me with your presence and speak words of hope into the dark corners of my soul. You meet my needs and give me joy. You wrap me in your love.

"I believe you'll draw my loved one back to you. But even if you don't, I trust you. Your love is enough to sustain me, and your companionship is too real, too personal, and too sweet to ever doubt you. Whatever happens, I'll love and serve you forever, because you bring me joy that transcends my circumstances."

Even though my heart was broken, I felt stronger than ever. I had Jesus, and Jesus had me.

David said in Psalm 119:71, "It is good for me that I have been afflicted, that I may learn Your statutes" (NKJV).

I said, "It is good for me that I have been afflicted, that I might learn you."

Prayer champion Andrew Murray, in his book, *Waiting on God*, describes what happens as we walk the hills and valleys of prayer. "At our first entrance into the school of waiting upon God, the heart is chiefly set upon the blessings which we wait for. God graciously uses our need and desire for help to educate us for something higher than we were thinking of. We were seeking gifts; He, the Giver, longs to give Himself and to satisfy the soul with His goodness."[8]

In God's gracious mercy, He drew my loved one to himself. He redeemed their life and the years the locust had eaten (Joel 2:25). He restored my relationship with my loved one too. Today, the sweet fellowship we enjoy as we walk the faith walk together brings me deep and abiding joy.

I don't ever want to experience sorrow like I endured in those dark years, but I'm grateful for it. It taught me lessons about God I couldn't have learned any other way. Best of all, it helped me realize that the greatest prize of all isn't the gift; it's the Giver.

Uncommon Power

Prayer lifts our eyes from the gifts we seek to the Giver of those gifts. There we find our greatest treasure.

Praise Prompt

Oh Father, how often I come to you seeking something when what I really need is Someone. *Thank you for teaching me that the greatest gift you can give me is you.*

Live It Out

When you come to God in prayer, what is the object of your desire? Don't feel guilty or less spiritual if the main reason you pray is because you need something. God invites us to bring our needs to Him. After you've shared your needs, look for evidence of His love and care for you. Write down these observations and think on them, allowing your love and gratitude for God himself to grow.

15

Persevering in Prayer

**Let us not become weary in doing
good, for at the proper time we will
reap a harvest if we do not give up.**

GALATIANS 6:9

Nestled in the folds of the Christmas story is a narrative that contains powerful hope for those of us who have prayed long about something with little or no visible results. Maybe we've prayed for a lost loved one, a difficult marriage, or a chronic health condition. We wonder if God hears our prayers. Sometimes we wonder if He cares. His silence and seeming lack of desire to change our situation make us weary and tempt us to give up. And yet we pray on.

The story of Zechariah and his wife, Elizabeth, reminds us that although God seldom works on our timetable, He always hears our prayers, and they never expire.

As the story begins, Zechariah the elderly priest has been given a once-in-a-lifetime opportunity to burn incense in the temple of the Lord. He was "righteous in the sight of God," the Bible tells us, "observing all the Lord's commands and decrees blamelessly" (Luke 1:6).

As he prepared to offer the fragrant incense to God, an angel appeared.

An angel.

Angels appear occasionally on the pages of Scripture. Familiarity often causes us to breeze right past them, but they weren't common in the first century. Four hundred years of silence echoed in the space between the final promise of Malachi and the first whisper of Matthew, but now the silence is over.

God picks up the conversation right where He left off—by heralding the forerunner of the Messiah. He sends an unexpected message to an unassuming man through an otherworldly messenger.

Did the angel's clothes shimmer with ethereal light from God's presence? Did he shake space dust from his garments? Did his feet shine with the reflection of golden pavement?

I've no doubt his appearance was awe-inspiring, because Scripture tells us Zechariah was "gripped with fear" (v. 12).

Maybe Zechariah reached for his nitroglycerin pills or leaned, trembling, on his staff. Perhaps he blinked his cataract-clouded eyes—more than once.

"Do not be afraid," the angel said, "your prayer has been heard" (v. 13).

My prayer? What prayer? Zechariah blinked again, this time in confusion.

"Your wife Elizabeth will bear you a son" (v. 13).

God heard my prayer for a son? I prayed that prayer every day for years. I cried. I begged. I fasted.

But that was decades ago. And when Elizabeth's womb remained empty and her fruitful years passed, he stopped praying. That dream died.

"You are to call him John. He will be a joy and delight to you, and many will rejoice because of his birth" (vv. 13–14).

Joy and delight.

The angel's words to Zechariah were a gift, just like the son that followed them nine months later. They are a gift to us as well.

They remind us there is no expiration date on our prayers. They go ahead of us into eternity. They continue to accomplish God's purposes long after the words leave our lips.

In the fullness of time and according to His good plan, God moves. This is why, in faith, we persevere in prayer.

God answered Zechariah's prayer decades after he had uttered it, but He didn't give him what he asked for.

He gave him so much more.

Instead of giving Zechariah an ordinary little boy who lived an ordinary little life, God gave him John the Baptist, the one who would come "in the spirit and power of Elijah, to turn the hearts of the parents to their children and the disobedient to the wisdom of the righteous—to make ready a people prepared for the Lord" (v. 17).

Our human understanding is limited and shortsighted. We ask for things that seem reasonable, and we often grow weary in the wait.

But God has greater plans. His understanding is boundless. His purposes are eternal. And His time frame spans generations.

We take the short view of today and tomorrow and next week. He takes the long view and sees into the end of time. We plant a faith seed today and expect to reap a miracle tomorrow. But Galatians 6:9

gives us solid ground on which to stand: "Let us not become weary in doing good, for at the proper time we will reap a harvest if we do not give up."

His plan of redemption and grace marches on, unaltered by human frailty and failure. God will rescue His people (Deuteronomy 32:36). He will complete the good work He has begun in us (Philippians 1:6).

And He will answer our prayers. Not always in the way we think. But in the way He knows is best and when the time is right.

Uncommon Power

Because our prayers have no expiration date, we can pray with perseverance, knowing we'll reap a spiritual harvest and eternal joy.

Praise Prompt

Oh Father, my heart fills with praise and gratitude at the way you fulfill your plans down through the ages. Even today, in my life, you are working out your good plan to draw me closer to yourself and fulfill your good purposes for my life. When I grow weary, remind me that I can trust you to accomplish all you have ordained, for my good and your glory. In Jesus's name I pray, amen.

Live It Out

What are you praying for today? What have you prayed for in the past and failed to receive? Zechariah's story reminds us that we can trust God not only to hear our prayers but to answer them—in His timing and in ways we could never have imagined.

16

Practicing the Discipline
of Thanksgiving

You crown the year with your bounty, and
your carts overflow with abundance.

PSALM 65:11

"This is the best day ever," my five-year-old granddaughter, Lauren, said, purple Popsicle juice dripping from her chin. "Thank you, Gigi."

Her simple declaration made me smile. *The best day ever.* And her gratitude warmed my heart.

Thinking back over the events of the day, I found nothing noteworthy. No great expenditure of money. No lavish displays of entertainment. No exotic travel or unusual events, just simple pleasures with someone she loved and a heart that overflowed with thanksgiving.

King David had a heart like Lauren's, and he expressed it in the grateful prayer we know as Psalm 65.

"Praise awaits you, our God, in Zion," he penned.

Then he listed what made his heart happy and full:

God hears our prayers (v. 2).

He atoned for our sins (v. 3).

He chose us to have a relationship with Him (v. 4).

He allows us unlimited access to His presence (v. 4).

He satisfies us with His goodness (v. 4).

He answers when we call (v. 5).

He is right in all His ways (v. 5).

He is our confidence (v. 5).

He is strong and powerful (v. 6).

He provides our needs (vv. 9–11).

"You crown the year with your bounty," David declared, "and your carts overflow with abundance" (v. 11).

David's thanksgiving prayer reminds me of a story I heard about an elderly man. Although he had few material possessions, he joyfully walked with God all the days of his life. As he prepared to eat his meager breakfast of coarse bread and cool water, he paused and bowed his head. He prayed from a heart overwhelmed by gratitude, "Oh Lord, you have given me bread and water, and Jesus too?"

Or, to borrow Lauren's words, "Fun Fridays with Gigi, and Popsicles too?"

Whether or not there's a Popsicle in your freezer, today is a good day to raise a prayer of thanksgiving to God. It's fitting to take a moment to praise Him for His attributes and thank Him for His goodness.

I've discovered that recognizing and appreciating God's goodness fills my heart and causes it to overflow in praise. I suspect, as Lauren's simple expression of gratitude warmed my heart, our thankful prayers make God smile.

It may even prompt us to declare, "This is the best day ever."

Uncommon Power

Prayers of praise and thanksgiving that flow from a heart filled with gratitude bless God and those around us.

Praise Prompt

Oh, Father, you have blessed us beyond what we deserve. You answer our prayers, atone for our sins, choose us to have a relationship with you, allow us unlimited access to your presence, and satisfy us with your goodness. We don't deserve your loving kindness, yet you pour it out upon us all the days of our lives. Accept our humble gratitude. You alone are worthy of praise.

Live It Out

Open your Bible to Psalm 65. Read it aloud to God, pausing between verses to ponder their meaning. Consider how they apply to your life. Allow your heart to mirror the gratitude in King David's heart as you praise our precious Lord and Savior.

Part 4

How Should
I Pray?

17

Praying in Light of God's Blessing

So God created mankind in his own image, in the image of God he created them; male and female he created them. God blessed them.

GENESIS 1:27-28

Seeing the sun and moon in the sky at the same time always surprises me. The sun shines brightly, illuminating all but the most sheltered corners of the landscape, while the moon emits its ghostly image somewhere above the horizon. As the sun eclipses the moon, the announcement that God has created man and woman in His image almost completely outshines the verse that follows: "God blessed them" (Genesis 1:28).

Yet this verse has the power to completely change how we approach God in prayer.

The verb *to bless*—*barak* in Hebrew—is the same word used to describe what God did after He created the seventh day. "Then God *blessed* the seventh day" (2:3). *To bless* means "to set apart or consecrate for holy purposes."

By blessing Adam and Eve, God set them apart.

He declared that their lives not only had purpose, but that purpose was special, holy, and God-ordained. The same is true of us. We, too, are created in God's image. We share Adam and Eve's blessing and are set apart for God-ordained purposes. Our lives are not random and purposeless.

How can this truth impact our prayer lives?

When we come to God in prayer knowing He has created us for a purpose, our hearts are positioned to work with Him to accomplish His good and perfect will in the world. As we obey His Word and the leading of His Spirit, we can be confident He'll fulfill His will—in us, for us, and through us.

Instead of approaching Him with ideas about what we think we should do, we can ask Him to reveal *His* will for us. We can pray for insight and direction. Since we've been created as part of His plan, if we obey what He calls us to do, we'll cooperate with Him to accomplish His purpose for our lives. As we seek God's will in prayer, we can trust Him, knowing He'll use the circumstances of our lives for our good and His glory.

Uncommon Power

Knowing God set us apart for His good purposes positions us to pray in cooperation with His plan to bless and use us to glorify himself.

Praise Prompt

I praise you, Father, for creating me in your image. Thank you for blessing me—setting me apart for your good purposes. What a joy to know my life isn't governed by chance, but by a loving, wise, trustworthy God. This brings me such peace. I will not fear the future, because my destiny rests safely in your hands. Help me bring you glory and point others to you. Amen.

Live It Out

Today as you approach God in prayer, instead of telling Him how to order the circumstances of your life, invite Him to work freely in those circumstances. Ask Him to give you the strength, determination, and faith to fulfill the God-ordained purpose for which He has set you apart. Whenever you see the moon and the sun in the sky together, remember not to allow the fact that God created you to eclipse the fact that He also blessed you.

18

Praying as a Beloved Child

Take delight in the LORD, and he will give
you the desires of your heart.

PSALM 37:4

In a scene from Charles Dickens's novel, *Oliver Twist*, dozens of orphaned boys sleep side by side in a long barrack. One boy, however, isn't sleeping. He paces the rows between the beds, clutching his growling belly.

"Lie down," one of his bunkmates grumbles. "You're keeping us all awake."

"I can't," he says. "I'm so hungry I'm afraid I might eat the boy beside me."

All the boys are hungry, so they devise a plan—one will ask for an additional serving of gruel at the end of the next meal. If he receives a favorable reply, the rest will also ask for additional food to satisfy their gnawing stomachs.

Oliver draws the short thread. At the next meal, he gobbles his meager ration and gathers his courage. The room grows silent as he makes the long walk to the head of the table. His spoon clatters in his bowl, betraying his trembling hands.

He feels the dining-room monitor's angry glare before he sees it. Who would dare break ranks and approach unsummoned?

"Please, sir," Oliver says, raising his beseeching eyes and his empty bowl, "I'd like some more."

The man's eyes widen at the audacity of his request.

"What?! What?!"

He lifts his cane and brings it down hard on the boy's back. Oliver flees, reprimanded for daring to ask for more than the minimum.

I've never been a starving, neglected child, but some days I pray like one.

I confidently approach my heavenly Father to ask for food, clothing, and necessities on the basis of Matthew 6:31–32: "Do not worry, saying, 'What shall we eat?' or 'What shall we drink?' or 'What shall we wear?' For the pagans run after all these things, and your heavenly Father knows that you need them."

I assume, rightly so, that it's okay to ask for what I need. First Timothy 6:8 tells us, "If we have food and clothing, we will be content with that."

But because this verse encourages me to be content with what God supplies, I feel guilty about asking Him for anything more. I don't expect a cane to fly out of heaven and beat me, but I do fear God's disapproving gaze.

"What?! What?! You ungrateful wretch. I've given you so much, and you dare to ask for more?"

I've come to realize, however, that this view of God is as warped as the philosophy that teaches the other extreme—that God wants to give everyone a Hummer, a mansion, and a million dollars. One view portrays God as a genie in a bottle who exists to fulfill my every wish. The other view portrays God as a miser who grudgingly dispenses only what I need to survive.

Both views are unbiblical and dangerous.

As I've learned more about God's heart and His nature, my tendency to pray minimalistic prayers has changed. The Bible reveals God as a Father who loves to give good gifts (not just gruel) to His children (James 1:17). He's a God who created all things for our enjoyment (1 Timothy 6:17) and who encourages us to "open wide your mouth and I will fill it" (Psalm 81:10).

God delights to give gifts that bring His children joy. He invites us to ask Him to provide what we yearn for. Psalm 37:4 says, "Take delight in the LORD, and he will give you the desires of your heart."

This doesn't mean God will give us everything our hearts selfishly desire, as if we have a charge card with no limit. Instead, as we seek to know Him, learn His ways, follow His precepts, and find our deepest satisfaction in Him, we'll begin to desire the things He desires. Moreover, He'll strengthen and confirm the godly desires He planted in our hearts when He created us.

Because He knows us best, we can trust Him with our needs and wants. We can come to God in prayer as a beloved child, finding confidence and fullness of joy.

Uncommon Power

We can bring all our needs and wants to God in prayer, knowing we are beloved children with a lavish Father.

Praise Prompt

Oh, Father, thank you for the freedom you have granted me to come boldly before your throne to ask you to meet my needs. And then, Father, you've also given me the freedom to ask you for more than just my needs. I can bring my hopes, dreams, and longings to you, knowing you will filter my requests through your fingers of love and give me exactly what I need to be in the center of your will. Thank you for allowing me to approach you in prayer as your beloved child. I love you. Amen.

Live It Out

Think about how you approach God in prayer. Do you feel free to bring your needs to God but hesitant to ask for your wants? Do you view Him as a miser who doles out the bare minimum or as a generous Father who loves to give good gifts to His children? Look up the verses referenced in this devotion and ask God to show you His heart toward you.

19

Prayers of Praise Help Us Battle the Bully

[The LORD] has sent me to . . .
provide for those who grieve in Zion—
to bestow on them a crown of beauty
instead of ashes, the oil of joy instead
of mourning, and a garment of praise
instead of a spirit of despair.

ISAIAH 61:1, 3

I suspect everyone has encountered a bully at least once in their life. My bully waited for me in the stairwell at school. I don't know why he singled me out among the hundreds of students who attended our school, but I suspect he chose me because I was skinny, nerdy, and quiet.

My dad found me crying in my bedroom after the second attack. I told him how the boy had trapped me in the corner of the stairwell and kicked me. The sea of students moving past us hid his actions, and no one came to my rescue.

As my dad listened to my story, his eyebrows scrunched together, and his eyes became slits. Wrapping his arms around me, he said five words that made me feel brave again.

"I'll walk you home tomorrow."

When the dismissal bell rang the next day, I made my reluctant way toward the second-floor stairway, heart pounding like a woodpecker on a tree. Sure enough, there was the boy, waiting in the bend of the stairwell.

And there was my daddy, standing at the bottom of the stairs. I started down, and he started up, head and shoulders above the crowd. I waved and called to him, and my attacker froze.

Taking the stairs two at a time, my dad scooped me up and carried me down the stairs and out the front door.

The bully melted into the crowd. I never saw him again.

The longer I live, the more I realize that there are bullies throughout life. Like my attacker, they wait in hidden corners and jump out at us when we least expect it. Financial trials, relationship difficulties, sickness, and loss beat us up and leave us hurting and afraid.

God, however, is our champion. Our heavenly Father towers above anything and everything that threatens us. Nothing touches us that He hasn't foreseen and allowed for His good purposes.

I forget this sometimes. I pray through my list of broken relationships, needy friends, and tragic circumstances, and I come away sadder and more depressed than when I began. This usually happens when I skip what is perhaps the most important aspect of prayer—praise.

Praise in its simplest form is ascribing to God the glory due to Him. When we praise God, we recount His mighty deeds and describe His awe-inspiring attributes.

God calls us to praise Him not because He's on some cosmic ego trip. He doesn't need to hear us describe how wonderful He is. We need to hear us describe how wonderful He is. When we declare that He is sovereign, good, patient, mighty, just, compassionate, forgiving, loving, and kind, we remind ourselves who orders our days and directs our lives.

Praise helps us see God in all His glory. When we see that He is head and shoulders above anything that threatens us, we can bring our needs to Him with confidence, knowing nothing is too hard for Him.

The bully in the stairwell frightened me until my dad showed up. When we begin our prayer times with praise, God shows up and the bully of discouragement vanishes. As we remind ourselves how big God is and realize we don't have to be afraid, we gain confidence that our heavenly Father will carry us through every trial until the day He takes us home to live with Him forever.

Then the praise will *really* begin.

Uncommon Power

Praise banishes the bully of discouragement and lifts our eyes to see the magnificence of our great Savior.

Praise Prompt

Father, I praise you for who you are. You are the creator and sustainer of all. You hung the stars and hold the world in place. You are stronger than anything that threatens me, and you are intimately acquainted with all my ways. Your sacrificial love purchased my salvation. Your sustaining grace enables me to face every day without fear. Great are you, Lord, and most worthy of praise.

Live It Out

Pray the words of Psalm 34 out loud to the Lord at the beginning of your prayer time today. Think on God's attributes and take comfort and courage from them. If you haven't done so already, develop the habit of beginning your prayer time each day by praising God for who He is and what He has done. Other psalms of praise include Psalms 89, 92, 95, 100, 103, and 111.

20

To Whom Should I Pray?

> Hear my cry for help, my King and my
> God, for to you I pray.

PSALM 5:2

"I know Jesus and God are the same person," my friend Mary said, "and we pray to God through Jesus, but I struggle to understand how my prayers get communicated to God and to know who I'm praying to."

I can relate to Mary's struggle. Most of my prayers begin with, "Heavenly Father," or "Dear God," but sometimes a "Dear Jesus" slips out. And what about the Holy Spirit? He's the third person of the Trinity and just as much God as the Father and the Son. Should we ever pray to Him?

If we think too long about the Trinity, how God is one yet three persons, we'll think ourselves into a headache. Scholars have unsuccessfully attempted to explain the unity and distinction of our triune God for millennia. Thankfully we don't have to resolve this issue to explore Mary's question.

Before Christ came, Old Testament priests offered sacrifices to God on behalf of the people to make temporary atonement for their sin. When Christ offered the ultimate sacrifice—His sinless body on the cross—He removed the veil that stood between man and God. He allowed His children to have unrestricted access to Him without a human mediator.

"For there is one God and one mediator between God and mankind, the man Christ Jesus" (1 Timothy 2:5).

No longer do we have to pray through a priest for the forgiveness of sins. We don't have to ask a saint or other person to pray for our needs. We can talk to God himself.

This brings us to the question, Which person of the Godhead should we pray to? Do the persons of God divide up prayer needs like departments in a retail store? The last thing we want to hear in response to our prayers is, "I'm sorry, that's not my department."

Whomever we address our prayers to, ultimately we pray to the one triune God. Sometimes, however, we might direct specific prayers to one particular member of the Godhead. The psalmist and most Old Testament saints directed most of their prayers to God the Father. They knew the Father promised to meet their needs, forgive their sins, grant them wisdom, and bring them peace. He is all-powerful, all-knowing, and the perfect manifestation of love. Like a good father, He cared about every detail of their lives and promised to care for them always. He deserved their worship and praise.

Sometimes I address my prayers to Jesus. Since I know Jesus the God-man walked the dusty roads of earth and struggled with temptation as I do, I find Him an empathetic listener. He experienced the pain of betrayal, the agony of rejection, and the frailty of His human body. He wept at a loved one's grave and laid a hand on a friend's fevered brow. He had to seek God for direction and power. Picturing Jesus's face when I pray reassures me of what I already know—that God, through Jesus, understands.

Other times, I pray to God the Holy Spirit. When Jesus ascended into heaven, He sent the Holy Spirit to "teach you all things and . . . remind you of everything I have said to you" (John 14:26). I learned early in my Christian life to invite the Spirit to be my teacher before I read the Scriptures or lead a Bible study.

I also ask the Holy Spirit to fill and empower me to do the things God calls me to do (Romans 8:11–13). As I pray for my lost loved ones and friends, I ask the Holy Spirit to open their eyes, convict them of their sin, and draw them to himself (John 16:7–8).

Ultimately, Christians direct their prayers to one source and one source only—God. Whether we speak to the person of God the Father, God the Son, or God the Holy Spirit, the result is the same. God Almighty hears our prayers. Aren't you glad?

Uncommon Power

Regardless of which member of the Trinity we pray to, God hears and moves in response to our prayers.

Praise Prompt

Father, how marvelous that in the three persons of the Trinity we find everything we need. You are our Creator, Savior, and Counselor. As our Father, you formed us from dust, breathed life into our bodies, and control our destiny. As the Son, you know what it means to be human. You sacrificed yourself to grant us eternal life and empathize with our frailties. As the Holy Spirit, you live within us, intercede on our behalf, and teach us all things. What a marvelous God you are! Amen.

Live It Out

Think a moment about how you pray. To which member of the Trinity do you typically address your prayers? Today, experiment with talking to each member of the Godhead. Offer praise and thanksgiving to God the Father, share your struggles and weaknesses with God the Son, and invite God the Holy Spirit to teach and empower you.

21

Why Pray in Jesus's Name?

**And I will do whatever you ask
in my name, so that the Father may
be glorified in the Son.**

JOHN 14:13

In my early days as a Christian, I learned by watching other believers. I found prayer especially fascinating. Every Wednesday night during prayer meeting, I'd hear people pray about specific needs or situations. The following week, they'd share how God had answered their prayers.

Like summoning Aladdin's genie, it seemed that some people knew just how to rub the bottle to get God to give them what they wanted. As I analyzed their prayers, I noticed, almost without exception, that each prayer ended with the words, "In Jesus's name I ask, amen."

This must be the ticket, I concluded. Ask for whatever you want, then end your prayer with "In Jesus's name I ask, amen." Or, like Brother Bill, say it real fast and smoosh the words together: "InJesus'snameIaskamen."

In the years since, I've learned a bit more about what it means to pray in Jesus's name. It's certainly not the magic formula I'd thought. It's a powerful mindset we can apply to our prayer lives.

Jesus invites us to pray in His name. "I will do whatever you ask in my name, so that the Father may be glorified in the Son" (John 14:13). Wow. That's quite a promise.

What does it mean to ask "in Jesus's name"?

It involves two things—position and purpose.

First, when we come to God in Jesus's name, we approach Him from our position as representatives of Christ, ambassadors. An ambassador is someone empowered to act on behalf of another. When we pray in Jesus's name, we say, in essence, "If Jesus were standing here, this is what He'd ask for."

My friend Frank is the CEO of a Fortune 500 company. He regularly borrows money on behalf of the company. Although he's not the owner, he has the authority to act in the owner's place. When Frank presents a request, the bank responds to him not on the basis of who he is, but on the basis of who the owner is. Frank serves as his representative.

As Christians, we've been given the authority to approach God's throne to make requests in accordance with Jesus's will. If you find this sobering, you're not alone. Approaching God as a representative of Jesus requires us to ask, "Would Jesus ask for this?" If the answer is no, God's answer will also be no.

So how do we know what Jesus would ask for?

We learn Jesus's will through His Word. The Bible teaches us what Jesus loves and what He hates. When we pray for the lost to be saved, believers to grow in their faith, good to triumph, and evil to be van-quished, we know we're praying according to Jesus's will.

The godly counsel of others, biblical resources, sermons, and Bible studies can be valuable sources of clarity as well. God says He will give us wisdom when we ask (James 1:5), and He often uses other believers to provide us with insight.

Jesus also reveals His will to us through the Holy Spirit, who lives within us. Sometimes the Spirit directs our prayers and leads us to petition God in ways we wouldn't have thought of on our own. Because we have the mind of Christ, His Spirit guides our prayers. When we don't know what to pray, the Holy Spirit intercedes for us (Romans 8:26).

The second thing to consider when praying in Jesus's name involves examining our purpose. Jesus invited His followers to pray in His name for one purpose only—"that the Father may be glorified."

In my early days of praying, this litmus test knocked out about ninety-nine percent of my requests. I wasn't concerned about what might glorify God. All I cared about was me—my comfort, my wishes, and my perspective.

As I've learned to seek God's glory, this change in perspective has refined and defined my prayers. When I pray for God to be glorified in every situation—knowing that each time He is glorified, others are drawn closer to Him—I can confidently pray, "Not my will, but yours be done. In Jesus's name I ask, amen."

Uncommon Power

Praying in Jesus's name involves accurately representing His wishes and asking for what will glorify God.

Praise Prompt

Oh, Father, what a privilege to be able to come to you in the precious name of Jesus! Help me consider my requests carefully, with your will in mind, so you'll be pleased to answer them. Thank you for the honor of praying in your name. Amen.

Live It Out

Before you pray, ask two questions: "If Jesus was standing before the Father, would He ask for this?" and "Will the answer to my request glorify God?" You may not be able to answer either question with certainty, but this practice will help you check your motives and eliminate some requests. Knowing your prayers honor Jesus and seek to glorify God will add power and confidence to your times of intercession.

22

What's Faith Got to Do with It?

Without faith it is impossible to please God, because anyone who comes to him must believe that he exists and that he rewards those who earnestly seek him.

HEBREWS 11:6

Picture the most beautiful car you've ever seen. Maybe it's the latest model Porsche or BMW. Perhaps a Lamborghini makes your heart beat hard. If you love American cars, a Chevy Camaro or Ford Mustang might fit the profile for your dream car. Regardless, it would have a leather interior and every gadget and comfort imaginable, custom built for you and your needs.

But how useful would your dream car be with no gas in the tank?

It would still look good. The surround sound stereo would still fill the car with music. The seats would feel comfy, and you could open the moon roof to get a glimpse of the stars.

But without gas, that sweet ride's going nowhere.

The same is true of our prayers. We can pray the most beautiful prayers—in reverent whispers or passionate shouts—or surround ourselves with Bible verses that wrap us in warmth and comfort. We can even catch glimpses of God's heavenly plans and power, but if our prayers aren't fueled by faith, they go nowhere.

"When you ask," James 1:6–7 says, "you must believe and not doubt, because the one who doubts is like a wave of the sea, blown and tossed by the wind. That person should not expect to receive anything from the Lord."

If faith makes the difference between answered and unanswered prayers, we need to know what faith is.

Faith, in its simplest form, is believing God is who He says He is, and that He can do what He says He can do. Hebrews 11:6 puts it this way: "Without faith it is impossible to please God, because anyone who comes to him must believe that he exists and that he rewards those who earnestly seek him."

Notice what the verse doesn't say: "You must summon up atomic reserves of energy and passion and believe with every brain cell and all your heart that God's going to do what you ask Him to do. And if you doubt, even for one nanosecond, you won't get what you ask for. Try again later."

Instead, Hebrews 11:6 says two things: believe God is real, and trust that He wants to reward you for seeking Him.

And lest you're tempted to get out your spiritual ruler and measure your faith against some imaginary or unattainable standard, remember that what matters most is not how much faith you have, but who you have faith in.

Do you remember the father who begged Jesus to heal his demon-possessed son?

"If you can believe," Jesus said, "all things are possible" (Mark 9:23 NKJV).

Admitting the frailty and desperation of his faith, the father cried out with tears, "Lord, I believe; help my unbelief!" (v. 24 NKJV).

The father didn't know if it was God's will to heal his son. Sometimes God has a greater work in mind in this world than alleviating our suffering, ending our trials, or curing our diseases.

But like the man who brought his son and his mustard seed faith to Jesus, we can come boldly before Him. We can acknowledge our trust in God's ability to answer our prayers and surrender our will to His will. We can trust Him to do what is best.

When my friend Jill prayed for a baby, she prayed in faith. "Lord, I know, based on Isaiah 66:9, that you have the power to open my womb and give me a child. You did it for Sarah and Hannah in the Bible, and you've done it for women down through the ages. If it's your will, please help me conceive. If you have another plan, a better plan that I can't see or imagine, I trust you. May your will be done. Amen."

Jill endured years of infertility, IVF treatments, miscarriages, and two failed adoption attempts.

And then came Marcus.

Premature, abandoned at the hospital by his mother, and unwanted by his father, he was a throwaway baby.

But not to God. And not to Jill and her husband, Tony. They fostered him, then adopted him. Now they can't imagine their lives without him.

"Our journey was excruciating," Jill told me. "But as we waited, God drew us closer to himself. He matured our faith and taught us to trust Him in so many ways. We'd resigned ourselves to the fact that we might never have a baby. If that was God's will for us, we knew He'd give us the ability to accept it and embrace it. Reaching that place in our faith walk was a gift."

"I learned to ask in faith," she said, "and trust His will."

Uncommon Power

To ask in faith, we must believe God can answer our prayers and trust Him to do what's best.

Praise Prompt

Lord, I want my prayers to be fueled by faith, but it's hard. I know in my head you know what's best for me, but my heart struggles to trust. Yet this is the essence of faith. Help me trust you more each day. Like a helpless baby, enable me to rest securely in your arms, confident in your love and wisdom. In the strong name of Jesus I pray, amen.

Live It Out

What are you praying for right now? Bring your request to God in faith (even if it's mustard seed–sized faith), then, with that same faith, surrender your will to His. He is worthy of your trust.

23

What's the Bible Got to Do with It?

For the word of God is alive and active. Sharper than any double-edged sword, it penetrates even to dividing soul and spirit, joints and marrow; it judges the thoughts and attitudes of the heart.

HEBREWS 4:12

My daughter and I were enjoying a lively phone conversation when I realized she hadn't spoken in a while. I shared a few more details of my latest project, then asked, "Are you still there?"

No response.

"Hellooooo? Can you hear me? Did I bore you to death or put you to sleep?"

Click.

The words *Signal lost* appeared on my screen.

I called her back and asked, "What was the last thing you heard before we were disconnected?" I was embarrassed to learn that I'd talked for several minutes with no one listening.

Do you ever feel this way about your prayers? I have.

I'll pray and pray and pray and get no response. Is God listening, or am I talking to myself?

My prayer life changed dramatically when I learned God intends prayer to be a two-way conversation. There's nothing wrong with pouring out our hearts to God. He encourages us to bring our thoughts, needs, and concerns to Him. Unfortunately, I was talking so much, God couldn't get a word in edgewise. I needed to listen at least as much as I talked.

One of the primary ways God speaks to us is through His Word. When I incorporated Bible reading into my prayer time, my somewhat-boring monologue transformed into a never-boring dialogue.

Each morning, I settle into my recliner and grab my prayer journal and my *One Year Bible. The One Year Bible* divides the Scripture into daily readings that include a passage from the Old Testament, a passage from the New Testament, a portion of a Psalm, and a few verses from Proverbs. Each selection takes about fifteen minutes to read. If I read every day, I can read the whole Bible in a year.

I begin my prayer time by reading from the Psalms. The psalms were the Israelites' hymns, and they invite us to praise and worship.

Next, I pray Psalm 139:23–24: "Search me, God, and know my heart; test me and know my anxious thoughts. See if there is any offensive way in me." As I quiet myself before Him, God often brings to mind the sins of the day before—an unkind word, a bad attitude, or outright disobedience to one of His commands. I confess and forsake each sin, asking God to forgive me and help me obey Him better.

After I praise Him and examine my heart for sins, I pray for the people on my prayer list. I date each request and leave space to record God's answers. My prayer journals have become a chronicle of my faith walk and a testimony to God's faithfulness.

When I finish praying through my list, I quiet myself and "listen" for God's response. While God could speak audibly to me, He never has. In this era, God speaks to believers primarily through His Word.

As I read the daily portion of Scripture, I "listen" with an ear toward how God might be responding to what I just prayed about.

James 1:5 promises God will give me wisdom if I ask for it. I often find the insight I need for the day in my daily Bible reading. Other times I find comfort, hope, instruction, truth, direction, or promises.

Sometimes God uses the Bible to remove an item from my prayer list by helping me realize what I'm asking for isn't His will for me. Other times He shares His heart. I read how He loves His children, longs to bless us, and grieves when we turn away from Him. As I spend time in prayer and Bible reading, God reveals more and more about himself, and I fall more and more in love with Him.

I encourage you not to be satisfied with a one-way conversation with God. Open your Bible and listen to Him speak. Your prayer life will never be the same again.

Uncommon Power

The God of the universe speaks to us every time we read His Word.

Praise Prompt

Father, thank you for speaking to us through your Word. What a treasure to have your wisdom, insight, and direction at our very fingertips. I praise you that every time I turn my heart toward you, you meet me there. Help me never take for granted the privilege of prayer, but to approach our time together as the most important appointment of my day, because it is. Amen.

Live It Out

During your prayer time today, follow the format I've outlined above. Praise God, confess your sins, and bring your needs to Him. Quiet your heart (and your mouth) so He can speak to you through His Word. Write down what you sense Him saying and think on it throughout the day.

24

Should We Ever Stop Praying?

Then Jesus told his disciples a parable to show them that they should always pray and not give up.

LUKE 18:1

Lily has loved to write since she was a teenager. "Lord," she's prayed for years, "help me publish a book that will point others to you." Almost a decade has passed, and although she's enjoyed some writing success, her dream of publishing a book seems no closer to fulfillment than when she first prayed about it. She wonders if she should quit asking God for something He seems unwilling to grant.

Lisa lives with a difficult husband. Angry and explosive, he loses his temper over the smallest things. Although he's been faithful to her and provides well for their family, his anger has been an unpleasant part of their relationship for thirty years. Every morning Lisa prays, "Lord, help him not get angry today." Sometimes it feels like her prayers work, and other times it seems as though she's never prayed. Maybe she should quit asking God for help.

Sherry has a prodigal son. For years she's watched him self-destruct. After ten years of praying for his salvation, she feels weary and discouraged. She wonders if her prayers are accomplishing anything. Maybe she should just give up.

Is it ever appropriate to stop praying? Is there ever a reason to cross unanswered requests off our lists or strike them from our prayer journals?

I think so. Let's consider several good reasons to stop praying.

1. We should stop praying when God clearly answers no. If you've been praying about a relationship with someone, and he gets married, you can safely stop praying. God has closed that door. If you interviewed for a job, and they hired someone else, it's time to redirect your petitions. Banging our heads against doors God has unequivocally closed is futile and foolish. It reveals a stubborn heart that thinks we know better than God what's best for us.

Lily's book manuscript was turned down by every publisher she submitted it to. Once she exhausted her sources for book publication, she realized God might have something else in mind for her words. She converted her chapters into articles and submitted them to magazine and online publications. Five of her articles have been published, reaching more than fifty thousand readers—far more than most books ever reach. Now, instead of praying for a book, she asks God to direct her to the readers who need her words.

2. We should stop praying when God removes our desire for the object of our prayers. Many times I've begun praying for something, only to find my desire lessening. Maybe I discover more information and realize it's not best for me. Other times my desire wanes until it fades away. When this happens, I can confidently stop praying about it.

Psalm 37:4 promises when I delight myself in the Lord, He'll give me the desires of my heart. While this sometimes means He'll give me what my heart desires, it usually means that He'll give my heart the desires He wants me to have. As I pray in faith and trust that God knows what's best for me, He molds my desires to fit His plans and purposes for my life. In love, He sometimes takes what looks desirable and rubs off the shine so I can see it as it truly is.

3. We should stop praying when God shows us a greater purpose for our situation. As Lisa faithfully prays about her husband's temper, he continues to have angry outbursts. Through the years, she's noticed that her prayers have changed. Instead of asking God to transform her husband's disposition, she finds herself praying more about her response to his outbursts.

"Lord," she prayed recently, "help me not to return evil for evil, but use a soft answer to turn away his wrath (Proverbs 15:1). Help me love my husband even when he acts unlovable, forgiving him as Christ has forgiven me. Protect my heart from bitterness."

Lisa's husband may always struggle with anger, but God can change him. Even if He doesn't, Lisa can grow closer to the Lord and become more like Christ through the struggle. By being open to more than one answer to her prayers, Lisa has experienced closeness and growth in her relationship with Christ that's even sweeter than a husband with a peaceful disposition.

Which brings us full circle to Sherry, the woman whose prodigal son desperately needs salvation. Should she stop praying for him after ten years with no apparent results?

Never.

Never. Never. Never.

Perhaps God intends to use her next prayer to crack open the door of her son's heart. God will save those He's set apart for salvation, and He invites us to partner with Him in prayer so we can share the joy of their new birth. Like a mother in agonizing labor, we must push through until that spiritual baby is born.

If you've been praying for something, and God has closed the door, it's okay to stop praying. If you've been praying for something, and God has changed your heart, it's okay to stop praying. If you've been praying for something, and God has shown you a different purpose for your request, it's okay to stop praying.

But if you're praying for a loved one's salvation, never, ever stop. While there is breath left in your body, pray on.

Uncommon Power

When God calls us to pray, sometimes we pray for a season. Other times we pray for a lifetime.

Praise Prompt

Father, I thank you for not only calling me to pray but giving me the stamina and determination I need to persevere. Help me know when you're leading me in another direction or closing doors. Thank you for loving those who are dear to me even more than I love them. Help me pray and trust, trust and pray. I love you, Lord Jesus. Amen.

Live It Out

Did God bring a prayer situation to mind as you read today's devotion? Ask Him to show you whether you should stop praying or continue to pray. May God give you clarity and confidence as you act upon His guidance.

25

Praying in Community

**He took Peter, John and James with him
and went up onto a mountain to pray.**

LUKE 9:28

Jesus told believers to pray alone, in our spiritual "closets," but He didn't intend for us to stay there.

Intimate, solo prayers form the backbone of our prayer lives, but corporate prayer—talking to God with one or two others or in a group—adds the sinews, tendons, and muscles to enable us to intercede effectively. In the next few devotions, we'll dive into how praying together enhances and refreshes our prayer lives.

As my youngest daughter prepared to leave for college three hundred miles away from home, I grew increasingly concerned for her safety and well-being. Would she grow or falter in her faith? Would she choose good friends? Study hard? Make wise decisions? The closer we got to the day of her departure, the more frightened I became.

I shared my fears with a dear friend and discovered she was struggling with similar concerns. I don't remember who said it, but one of us had a flash of inspiration we credit to the Holy Spirit.

"Why don't we meet together once a month to pray for our kids?" We agreed and set a date.

But it didn't stop there.

"If we're feeling this way," I said, "we're not alone. Why don't we invite other moms to pray with us?" We spread the word, and Praying Parents was born.

Our Praying Parents group has prayed together now for more than a decade. We've prayed our kids through freshman years, midterms, finals, and graduation. Through licensing boards, job interviews, and grad school. Through dating, breakups, marriage, pregnancy, and parenthood. We began as praying moms. Now many of us are praying grandmas.

Although Jesus didn't have physical children, and certainly wasn't a grandma, His example encourages us to pray together. He walked the dusty roads of earth and modeled what it means to "pray continually," alone and with others. When He taught His disciples to pray, He used words suitable for corporate intercession. "*Our* Father in heaven . . . Give *us* today *our* daily bread . . . Forgive *us our* debts . . . Lead *us* not into temptation" (Matthew 6:9–13).

He took Peter, James, and John with Him on a mountainside to pray (Luke 9:28), and even when He prayed alone, His disciples were with Him (Luke 9:18).

When Jesus returned to heaven, the disciples continued to pray together.

"They all joined together constantly in prayer" (Acts 1:14).

"They raised their voices together in prayer to God" (4:24).

"They presented these men to the apostles, who prayed and laid their hands on them" (6:6).

"Peter was kept in prison, but the church was earnestly praying to God for him" (12:5), and when he miraculously escaped, he found "many people had gathered and were praying" (v. 12).

Even in jail, "Paul and Silas were praying and singing hymns to God" (Acts 16:25).

During more than a decade of praying together, our group of praying moms has experienced what Jesus's disciples did:

- The Holy Spirit's empowerment to love and serve God better (Acts 4:31).
- Wisdom and direction (Colossians 1:9).
- Deliverance for our loved ones from the forces of evil (Acts 12:11).
- Confidence to commit those we love to God (Acts 13:3).
- Joy in the midst of trials (Acts 16:25).
- Unity and love (Acts 1:14; 21:5–6).

Sometimes when I pray alone, I grow weary. My faith wobbles, and I forget the miraculous things God has done. I become so overwhelmed with my burdens that I can't see past them to God's throne. I fail to remember that nothing is too hard for God. That He hears and answers prayers. That the prayer of the righteous is powerful and effective (James 5:16). My sisters in Christ raise my weary arms and pray with me and for me. They shoulder the burdens I cannot carry alone.

And when an answer comes? They rejoice with me. When God brought salvation to my daughter and son-in-law, my joy overflowed and splashed onto them. God had used their prayers to accomplish something miraculous, and they knew it. They celebrated with exceeding joy at what God had done. Their faith grew stronger, because the same God who had saved my loved ones could save theirs as well.

Private, intimate prayer with God should be a daily part of our Christian lives. But if we stop there, we fail to experience the unifying, dynamic, soul-stretching joy of praying with other believers.

Uncommon Power

Praying with others strengthens our resolve to pray and reinforces our faith.

Praise Prompt

Father, thank you for placing us into a faith family when you called us to yourself. I praise you that you never intended for us to do life alone. You gave us the Holy Spirit, and then you gave us each other—brothers and sisters in Christ—to walk out this faith journey. Thank you for the joy and power of praying with and for each other. In Jesus's precious name I pray, amen.

Live It Out

Is there a kindred spirit in your life with whom you could pray? Someone who loves God and is committed to prayer? Is there a group of people who believe God works through prayer? Why not reach out? Connect with them, either in person or online. Commit to carrying each other's burdens to God in prayer—together (Galatians 6:2).

26

The Beauty and Power of a Prayer Chorus

**I urge you, brothers and sisters, by our Lord
Jesus Christ and by the love of the Spirit, to
join me in my struggle by praying.**

ROMANS 15:30

During my years of church membership, I've sung soprano in two choirs. I'm not soloist material, but I've sung when no one more gifted was available. I prefer to join my voice to the voices of others rather than sing by myself. The same is true of my prayer life.

When Christ returned to heaven after His resurrection, He gave the church—the body of believers—the biblical mandate to "go and make disciples of all nations, baptizing them in the name of the Father and of the Son and of the Holy Spirit, and teaching them to obey everything I have commanded you" (Matthew 28:19–20). We can't fulfill this world-changing mission without prayer. And not just individual prayer but corporate prayer—bringing our requests to God in concert with other believers.

Group prayer is found throughout the Bible. Esther, Ezra, and Nehemiah called God's people to pray as a community. After Christ ascended, the early church prayed together. They asked God for wisdom, protection, power, and deliverance. Today, two thousand years after Christ's resurrection and two thousand years closer to His return, we have even more reason to pray. Earnestly and corporately, we ask for God's will to be done on earth as it is in heaven.

In the previous devotion, I shared an example of how I pray with a small group of friends. God also calls us to pray together as the body of Christ—the church. Praying with the church, local or universal, enables us to experience five things we'd miss if we only prayed alone.

First, corporate prayer promotes unity among believers. When we pray together—for the ministries of the church, the needs of others, and the church's global mission—our hearts bond. We connect because common goals, concerns, and passions unite us. Like teammates dedicated to vanquishing our opponent and winning the victory, we rally around God's cause and become inspired to work together to accomplish it.

Second, it fosters love and compassion. Theologian William Law observed, "There is nothing that makes us love a man so much as praying for him."[9] As we lift each other's needs to God, compassion blossoms into the twin flowers of sympathy and empathy. We catch glimpses of each other's hearts. As we hear fellow Christians bare their souls to God, we can't help but fall in love with the Jesus we see in them.

Third, it leads to a more fruitful ministry. The apostle Paul often reminded the church to pray for his gospel work (Romans 15:30; 2 Corinthians 1:11; Ephesians 6:18–20). He could have prayed for his own needs (I'm sure he did), but he knew he'd experience greater fruitfulness if the church upheld him in prayer.

Fourth, it multiplies God's glory. Paul asked the Corinthian church to pray for God to protect and deliver him as he ministered. "On him we have set our hope that he will continue to deliver us, as you help us by your prayers. Then many will give thanks on our behalf for the gracious favor granted us in answer to the prayers of many" (2 Corinthians 1:10–11). Paul knew if the church labored together in prayer, they'd also rejoice and tell others when God answered their prayers. This is how we glorify God—by telling others what He has done. The more people who pray, the more people who can glorify God when the answer comes.

Finally, corporate prayer helps us grow spiritually. When I hear others pray and see how God responds, my faith grows. I remember that the same God who answered their prayers can answer mine. I see how God not only hears but moves in response to His children's requests. When someone references a passage of the Bible or prays the words of one of the heroes of the faith, I learn how to pray biblically. When I listen to another believer praising God's strength, kindness, love, and compassion, my view of God enlarges, and I fall further in love with Him.

A dynamic prayer life begins by spending private time with God every day, but it shouldn't end there. Like members of a choir, we should join our voices with others until our prayers become a beautiful, powerful chorus that brings joy to God's ears.

Uncommon Power

God calls us to pray together as a church to glorify himself and grow our ministries, our faith, and our hearts.

Praise Prompt

Father, even the mighty apostle Paul recognized that he needed the prayers of others. Thank you for sending other believers to strengthen us by praying for and with us when we grow weary in the battle of life. Thank you for reminding me today of the beauty and power of corporate prayer. Help me be more committed to praying with other believers. In Jesus's name I ask, amen.

Live It Out

Does your church pray together? Do you faithfully attend and participate in church-led times of prayer? Why or why not? Has today's devotion caused you to think differently about the value of praying together? If you don't already, commit to participate when an opportunity to pray corporately arises. If your church doesn't pray together, what can you do to change this?

27

Is Your Group Prayer Time Barren or Blessed?

**Peter was kept in prison, but the church
was earnestly praying to God for him.**

ACTS 12:5

As a new believer, I found midweek prayer meetings some of the least exciting services of all. Usually someone would present a short Bible lesson, which I enjoyed, then segue into the prayer portion of the evening.

"Does anyone have a request to share?" the pastor would ask. Miss Hildegarde would mention her bursitis, Mr. Bill would describe his neighbors' recent argument in colorful detail, and Miss Winnie would tell us to "remember the missionaries around the world." Occasionally a juicy snippet of gossip, sanctified by the words, "I hate to mention this, but so-and-so needs our prayers," would raise pious heads and eyebrows.

"Sharing" time would meander its way through family troubles, church ministry squabbles, and the latest political scandal. Finally the pastor would end the exchange by proclaiming the blessed words, "Let's go to the Lord in prayer." With only a few minutes of the hour left, he'd speak a blanket prayer over the requests and conclude with a hearty, "In Jeeeeesus's name I pray, amen."

I believe the faithful members who attended prayer meeting each week were well-meaning and sincere. Over the years, however, I've come to realize we probably didn't use our time as efficiently or effectively as we could have.

From the time Christ walked the earth, the church has prayed together. God has used the communal prayers of the saints to save lost souls, heal the sick, and turn the hearts of kings. When Peter was imprisoned, the church prayed as Jesus had taught them—together and in faith—for his deliverance. Again and again the apostle Paul implored fellow believers to pray for his gospel work.

Unfortunately, many of our gatherings bear little resemblance to the prayer meetings of old that sparked seasons of revival and summoned angel warriors to rescue God's servants.

If your church or small group struggles, like mine did, with meandering and ineffective prayer times, these five guidelines might help:

1. *Begin with God's Word.* Many come to prayer time discouraged and emotional. Opening with Scripture reminds us of the unseen Listener at every gathering. Hearing appropriate promises and verses reminds us we are in God's presence at His invitation and welcomes His voice into the conversation. Bible verses and passages remind us of God's heart and will in each situation and opens the door for the Holy Spirit to speak.

2. *Limit sharing time.* Although this seems counterintuitive, when we spend more time talking about our prayer requests than praying about them, we misuse our time. We appreciate the sympathy and emotional release we gain from sharing all the details of a troubling situation, but praying about the need can accomplish far more. To make the best use of your group's time, consider collecting prayer requests before you meet, either on slips of paper or a running prayer list. Or encourage your members to share their requests as they pray, giving only enough detail to help others pray along.

3. *Keep prayers brief and focused.* Group sessions aren't the time for each person to pray their way around the world. Choose a few specific needs and voice them in simple language and clear requests. Mention people, especially the lost, by name when appropriate. Consider inviting members to pray one-sentence prayers of praise, request, or thanksgiving. Resist the urge to pray to impress. Skip the grandiose words, and talk to God like a person—a person who loves you.

4. *Rein in your thoughts.* My mind often wanders while another person is praying. Perhaps something they're praying about reminds me of a need in my life. Other times my thoughts drift to the events of the day or what I ate for dinner. A wise pastor once said, "If you're thinking about anything other than what the person is praying about, you're not praying with them. You're just sitting in the same room." To avoid

distraction, we must train our minds to pray (silently) along with the person praying, echoing their prayers and helping them lift their requests before God.

5. *Come to God together.* Although prayer is all about talking to God, praying corporately invites others into the conversation. By using words like *we, us,* and *our,* we make our prayers inclusive. We come before Him united in heart and mind, committed to wrestling through every situation that needs our Father's help—together.

I find great comfort in knowing our prayers don't have to be perfectly executed or eloquent for God to respond. He hears every whisper and sigh we direct His way. At the same time, we must steward the time set aside for corporate prayer and maximize its effectiveness for the kingdom. Like the faithful saints who prayed for Peter's deliverance, we want to pray the type of prayers God is pleased to answer. In every church and gathering, He wants to set prisoners free.

Uncommon Power

When group prayer meetings are focused and intentional, it allows more room for the Holy Spirit to work, making our prayer times all the more blessed and fruitful.

Praise Prompt

Father, every minute in your presence is precious. What an honor to have an audience with you whenever we call upon your name. Help us pray with fervent, focused attention, then wait with expectation to see how you will answer our prayers. May every prayer we pray bring you glory. In Jesus's name I ask, amen.

Live It Out

When you gather with others to pray, is your time barren or blessed? If it's not everything it could be, which of these five suggestions might help? Perhaps these ideas have sparked some of your own. Prayerfully (and tactfully) apply them to your next group prayer time or share them with your prayer leader. Do what you can to make the most of your time together.

28

Don't Just Pray *For*, Pray *With*

**Encourage each other and build each
other up, just as you are already doing.**

1 THESSALONIANS 5:11 (NLT)

I've never had a panic attack, but one day I came close. I'd received a phone call informing me that someone I loved was walking through deep waters. Like snarling dogs surrounding a kitten, danger encircled her, threatening to destroy her and her family.

I've seldom felt fear like I did that day. My heart raced, and my mind swirled with terrifying what-ifs. I felt as though I were suffocating. As I paced in frantic circles trying to relieve the tension, the walls of my home hemmed me in like a cage.

Desperate for an outlet for the emotions churning inside me, I laced up my tennis shoes and headed outside. Maybe walking would help. I settled into my familiar path around the streets and cul-de-sacs of my neighborhood, my heartbeat keeping time with my feet.

What if she's not okay? What will happen to her family? Who will care for her children? Instead of quieting, my mind screamed like an engine pushed to its limits. I wanted to pray, but I couldn't form the words. Then a thought cut through the storm raging in my mind.

Call Charlotte. She'll understand.

My friend Charlotte is a prayer warrior who has navigated some of the deepest trials imaginable and come through with her faith intact.

My trembling fingers found her number, dialed, and waited. Mercifully, she answered on the second ring.

"Charlotte, this is Lori. I need you to pray." Fear constricted my throat, and I could barely squeeze the words out. Like an asthmatic during an attack, I struggled to breathe.

When my words slowed, I heard her Southern drawl through the phone. "Well, honey, let's pray."

I don't remember what she said that morning, but I'll never forget the peace that settled over me as she prayed. The band that had squeezed my heart all morning slowly loosened. My pounding heart settled into a normal rhythm. The tears that dampened my cheeks slowed to a trickle.

Someone who understood my pain was lifting my needs to the Father's throne. Someone who knew God intimately was standing in the gap for me. As Charlotte's soothing voice prayed God's promises over me, she reminded me of the truth I knew but had lost sight of. My tilting world righted, and my heart found courage.

Charlotte could have listened sympathetically, quoted a few Bible verses, and told me she'd pray for me, but she went one step further. She prayed *with* me. She stopped what she was doing (I never asked her if this was a convenient time to talk) and took my need to the Lord.

Because she knew what it felt like to fear for a loved one's well-being, she prayed with insight and empathy. She entered into my suffering, took the burden from my shoulders, and placed it on her own. I was too weak to carry my fears to the Lord, so she carried them for me.

Nothing immediately changed in my loved one's circumstances when Charlotte prayed, but something changed in my heart. Courage filled the trembling spaces. Peace quieted my soul. Hope flickered like a candle in the darkness.

Prior to that day, I'd listen to people's prayer needs and respond with, "I'll pray for you." Now, like my friend Charlotte, I pray *with* them.

I've prayed with patients in my dental chair as they faced a frightening procedure. I've prayed for students at the university as they take final exams. I've prayed for friends facing tests, biopsies, and cancer. I've prayed for neighbors hunting for lost pets. Whenever someone shares a need with me, if at all possible, I respond with, "Let's pray right now."

I'll never know the effects of my prayers, but if they bring a measure of hope and comfort to a struggling soul and remind them that God is near, they've accomplished their purpose. And I've fulfilled mine.

Uncommon Power

Praying *with* someone lightens their burden and strengthens their faith.

Praise Prompt

Father, thank you for calling us to pray for and with each other. Thank you for raising up intercessors to come alongside those who are struggling and lift their burdens. Give me the courage to pray with others—out loud—when they share their prayer needs with me. Use my prayers to fill them with hope and point them to you, our greatest source of comfort and strength. In the name of the Lord Jesus Christ I pray, amen.

Live It Out

Has someone ever prayed aloud with you? How did it make you feel? When people share prayer requests, how do you respond? Do you usually pray right then, aloud, in their presence, or tuck the request away to pray later? If you hesitate to pray aloud, identify what holds you back. What do you think God thinks about these concerns? Commit today, the next time someone shares a concern, to pray aloud with them. The more often you do it, the less scary it will become.

29

Prayer Shouldn't Be Boring

My mouth is filled with your praise, declaring your splendor all day long.

PSALM 71:8

Sometimes prayer is boring.

There. I said it. Are you shocked? I'm just being honest here. And if you're honest, you'll probably agree. As lofty and magnificent as it is to pray to the God of the universe, if we do it often enough, sometimes our prayer times can grow a little, well, stale.

You might, as I do, use a prayer journal to list the people and ministries you want to pray for. Or maybe you have a structure for your time of intercession, like one of my favorites, PART—Praise, Admit, Request, Thanksgiving. You might have a simpler method, like praying daily for your family, friends, and missionaries. However you structure your prayer time, if you pray often, you probably battle boredom from time to time.

Several years ago, during a season of unemployment, my husband, David, and I started walking together in the mornings. In all our thirty-plus years of marriage, we've never had schedules that allowed time to exercise together, but for three months we walked for an hour every morning. While we walked, we prayed.

After a few weeks, I noticed we were praying the same prayers, in the same order, for the same people, day after day. I knew repetition was necessary, but boredom was not. We put our heads together and brainstormed ways to infuse new life and joy into our times of intercession.

Whether you pray regularly with a partner or alone, these three practices can help jazz up your prayer time.

1. Use the alphabet to praise God.

David and I began most of our prayer times by praising God. Reminding ourselves of who God is reminds us that He is quite capable of answering our prayers and working on our behalf. Using the alphabet, we listed a character quality or attribute of God for every letter (*X* is tough). Then we turned each attribute into something for which to praise Him.

Here's an example: "God, you are our Advocate. Thank you for interceding for us when we're unable to help ourselves. You are also Benevolent, providing all we need, every day, in just the right amounts. I praise you for being Compassionate. You are a God who feels our pain, sympathizes with our weaknesses, and collects our tears in a bottle . . ."

The psalmist prayed, "My mouth is filled with your praise, declaring your splendor all day long" (Psalm 71:8).

2. Use the alphabet to pray for people.

Like chronicling the attributes of God with the ABCs, praying for people using the alphabet can also take your prayer time in a fresh new direction. Use the sequence of letters to prompt you to pray for a person whose name (first or last) begins with that letter.

Here's an example: "Father, today I'd like to pray for Aaron. Strengthen him in his faith. Help him love his wife as Christ loves the church. Help him parent his daughter wisely, and bless their unborn baby. Be with Bethany too. Help her grow to love you more and more. Inspire her to read her Bible every day and work hard in school. Thank you, Father, for Chris. Draw him to yourself. Save him and make him a mighty man of God for your glory."

3. Pray for people for whom you don't regularly pray.

The only rule for this prayer approach is that you can't have prayed for the person recently. Ask God to bring people to mind, and then pray for them as the Spirit leads you. When my husband and I pray this way, we're always amazed at the people who pop into our minds—friends we went to church with twenty years ago, other people's children, even patients of mine.

Trusting that the Lord knows these people need special prayer, we lift each one to the Lord. We'll probably never know how God used our prayers, but we can be confident that He took note of them and answered their needs appropriately.

God calls us to prayerful persistence, and oftentimes such repetition can be a little dull. Thinking creatively and mixing up our routine every now and then can renew our enthusiasm. If your prayer life needs a spark, I encourage you to try one of these ideas or brainstorm one of your own.

Uncommon Power

Our daily prayer time doesn't have to be boring. With a little creativity, our times of intercession can be fun and energizing.

Praise Prompt

Father, every opportunity I have to pray to you is a precious gift. I don't ever want to take this for granted. Help me expend the same creative effort in my conversations with you as I do with others I care about. Lift my eyes above the ordinary so I can see you in all your glory and magnificence. Help me articulate that wonder as I raise my voice in praise and thanksgiving. Help me never grow so comfortable in my prayer life that I cease to marvel at your willingness to hear and answer my prayers.

Live It Out

Have you struggled with boredom in your prayer life? Today, why not try one of the suggestions mentioned above or brainstorm another idea? Interaction with God should be intimate and dynamic. Don't settle for boring prayer times.

30

Spiritual Muscle Memory

Pray without ceasing.

1 THESSALONIANS 5:17 (NKJV)

When I met Elmer Thompson, I never dreamed the slightly forgetful octogenarian would become one of my heroes. As my husband and I transported him and his wife, Evelyn, to church, we learned they had served as missionaries in Cuba for decades. They founded a mission organization that supports more than ninety missionaries in two dozen countries. In his late eighties, he still knocked on doors in his neighborhood handing out gospel tracts.

By the time I met him, he was frail, white-haired, and sometimes confused. Although he'd been a passionate and fearless man during Castro's Cuba, all I saw was a stoop-shouldered, shuffling grandfather whose hearing aids didn't always work.

One Wednesday I asked him how he'd spent his day.

"On Wednesdays I pray for the missionaries in our organization," he said, his watery blue eyes sparkling behind his glasses. "I pray for each one of them by name. My son, Paul, leads our organization now. He's one of our missionaries." He cut his eyes at me, and I swear I saw him wink. "I pray for *him* every day."

I met Paul several months later, and he confirmed that his father had prayed for him and his siblings every day for as long as he could remember. "Whenever we visit Dad and get ready to leave, he prays over us. It's a gift."

I didn't see Paul again until he spoke at his father's funeral. He shared how dementia had muddied his father's mind and erased large parts of his memory. "The last time I visited him," he said, "Dad didn't say much. I thought he recognized me, but I couldn't be sure. He always asked me where I was traveling to next, but that day he just sat there, hunched over in his wheelchair, picking at a loose thread on the blanket that covered his lap.

"When I got ready to leave, I laid a hand on his shoulder and said, 'I love you, Dad.' He didn't respond, so I walked to the door." Paul paused, took a deep breath, and continued. "I turned back to look at my dad one more time. His eyes were closed, and I assumed he'd nodded off. But then I noticed his hands. They were folded in his lap, and his lips were moving.

"My dad didn't even remember his name," he said, shaking his head, "but he remembered to pray for me."

Paul's last memory of his father memorializes the habit Mr. Thompson developed over a lifetime—to "pray without ceasing." He prayed for missionaries, for friends, and for his family. He repeated the action so many times it became woven into the fabric of his days. When his mind failed, his spiritual muscle memory took over and carried him to the finish line.

Only heaven will reveal how many people were impacted by Mr. Thompson's prayers. Twenty years later, his mission organization has more than 350 missionaries serving in twenty-eight countries. All four of his children continue to serve God and live for Him. Hundreds of people like me who shared a bit of his life have been challenged to follow his example of habitual prayer. May God find us equally faithful.

Uncommon Power

No matter your age, you can strengthen your spiritual muscle memory now and develop a habit of prayer that will carry you through the rest of your life and leave an example for others to follow.

Praise Prompt

Father, I praise you for the ministry of intercession and for the privilege of partnering with you to accomplish your work in the world. Thank you for calling faithful intercessors to battle on their knees on our behalf. Raise up a new generation of prayer warriors to fill the ranks of spiritual soldiers in your army. How magnificently humbling it is to know that the effective, fervent prayer of a righteous person accomplishes much.

Live It Out

Brainstorm a plan to pray regularly for family, friends, and others. Use a prayer journal, index cards, sticky notes, or a phone app. Designate certain days for certain people groups. (On Monday pray for missionaries, Tuesday for your kids' or grandkids' teachers, Wednesday for pastors and teachers, etc.). Start your habit of praying now, and don't stop.

Part 5

What Should
I Pray For?

31

The Prayer God Always Says Yes To

Everyone who calls on the name of the Lord will be saved.

ROMANS 10:13

I prayed quite a few prayers before I became a Christian. As a child, I memorized and recited a few in an attempt to earn God's favor and pay penance for my sins. My heart still hurts to think I grew up equating prayer with punishment, like writing *I will not talk in class* a hundred times on the board at school.

I assumed God heard my prayers. He even appeared to respond to a few dramatic pleas for help in my teenage years. But it wasn't until the summer before my freshman year in college, while talking with my pastor, that I knew for sure He'd answered one of my prayers.

"God," I said, with tears of genuine repentance over my sin, "I've been living my life my way, and I've made a mess of it. I don't want to be in charge any longer. Please take control of my life. I surrender it to you. In Jesus's name I pray, amen."

When I opened my eyes, all I saw was my pastor's gentle smile. No doors in heaven opened, and no angelic choirs proclaimed, "Hallelujah." No heavenly chimes sounded. I looked exactly the same when I left my pastor's office as when I walked in.

But on the inside, something had changed. I knew as certainly as I knew my name that God had answered my prayer of surrender.

Until we yield our lives to God—and really mean it—we cannot pray with confidence. God promises to work on behalf of His children, not those who choose to live independently of (and, dare I say, rebelliously toward) Him.

Yet there is one prayer He always says yes to. Whether spoken by a tiny child during nighttime devotions or a cynical old man languishing on his deathbed, God always hears and answers the prayer of a repentant heart.

"Lord, be merciful to me, a sinner."

Have you ever prayed this prayer?

Do you feel shame and regret because you've lived your life in disregard (or outright disobedience) to God? When you lie in bed at night, do you wish you had a chance to start over? Do you long for your life to have meaning, purpose, and peace? Have you thought about heaven, hell, and where you'll spend eternity? Have you found no sure answer?

This, my friend, is the work of the Holy Spirit. God sent Him into the world to convict mankind of sin and of righteousness (John 16:8). To stimulate our hunger for Him. To make our hearts restless for more than this world offers. If you're experiencing these thoughts and feelings, God is wooing you to himself. Were it not for His compassionate work in your heart, you'd be deaf to His voice and blind to His love.

As God through Paul declared, "'In the time of my favor I heard you, and in the day of salvation I helped you.' I tell you, now is the time of God's favor, now is the day of salvation" (2 Corinthians 6:2).

But we can't come to God clinging to our old life. Like the thief crucified with Jesus, we must acknowledge our sin and forsake it. Only then can we ask for God's mercy.

"Then [the thief] said, 'Jesus, remember me when you come into your kingdom.' Jesus answered him, 'Truly I tell you, today you will be with me in paradise'" (Luke 23:42–43).

If you haven't come to God for salvation, then all your other prayers are useless. If you have, oh, the gracious favor that God extends toward you. As eighteenth-century preacher Charles Spurgeon declared, "Among the lost souls in hell, there is not one that can say, 'I went to Jesus, and He refused me.'"[10]

"Whoever comes to me I will never drive away," Jesus promised (John 6:37).

"Everyone who calls on the name of the Lord will be saved" (Romans 10:13).

Not only will God hear and answer your prayer for salvation, He promises that He has "turned his ear" toward every other prayer you speak, all the days of your life (Psalm 116:2).

Uncommon Power

God never refuses the prayer that springs from a broken and repentant heart.

Praise Prompt

Father, I praise you for making it possible for us to have a relationship with you. Jesus, thank you for extending your nail-scarred hands to us and drawing us into your family. Help me surrender my will to yours every day, trusting you to answer my prayers in the way that is best. I love you. Amen.

Live It Out

Without a relationship with God, we have no grounds from which to pray. If you've never confessed and forsaken (turned your back on) your sin and asked Christ to be your Savior, what are you waiting for? Talk to God in your own words. Accept His offer of salvation.

If you already have a relationship with God, are you fully surrendered to Him? Do you follow Him as best you know how? If not, talk to God about anything that stands in your way. Rest in the confidence that God will hear and answer your prayer.

32

Why God Says,
"I Promise"

His divine power has given us everything
we need for a godly life through our knowledge of him who called us by his own glory
and goodness. Through these he has given
us his very great and precious promises.

2 PETER 1:3-4

Have you ever wondered why God filled the Bible with promises? Estimates vary on the exact number, but even a casual student realizes the Bible includes thousands of promises from God to people. The word *promise* itself occurs more than two hundred times.

Did God make promises so we'd have something to hold over His head and force Him to do what He doesn't want to do? I remember pestering my dad for weeks to race me around the apartment building. Feeling frustrated because he'd put me off and sensing his reluctance, I played my trump card: "But you prommmmmmised."

The Bible tells us God makes promises for four reasons: to help us understand His nature, to guide us into His will, to strengthen our faith, and to help us pray with confidence.

Promises help us understand His nature. When I read Romans 10:9, "If you declare with your mouth, 'Jesus is Lord,' and believe in your heart that God raised him from the dead, you will be saved," I learn God wants to rescue me from my sin. When I read 1 John 1:9, "If we confess our sins, he is faithful and just and will forgive us our sins and purify us from all unrighteousness," I discover He's eager to forgive and wants to help me live a pure life. John 3:16 tells me God loved the world so much He sacrificed His only Son to make eternal life possible. Hebrews 13:5, "Never will I leave you; never will I forsake you," reveals His faithfulness and steadfast love. God's promises show us His nature and reveal His heart.

Promises also help us know God's will. The promise of Matthew 6:33, "Seek first his kingdom and his righteousness, and all these things will be given to you as well," calls me to make God the center of my life. First John 2:1, "My dear children, I write this to you so that you will not sin. But if anybody does sin, we have an advocate with the Father—Jesus Christ, the Righteous One," warns me to avoid sin and promises the Holy Spirit will help me when I mess up. Ephesians 6:1, 3—"Children, obey your parents in the Lord . . . 'so that it may go well with you and that you may enjoy long life on the earth'"—tells me God cares how I treat my parents. God's promises reveal His will; they don't coerce Him to submit to ours.

Promises strengthen our faith. God wants us to believe His Word and act in faith. When I respond to Philippians 4:6–7, "Do not be anxious about anything, but in every situation, by prayer and petition, with thanksgiving, present your requests to God. And the peace of

God, which transcends all understanding, will guard your hearts and your minds in Christ Jesus," my faith grows. When I give generously the way Philippians 4:19 commands, I learn that "God will meet all [my] needs according to the riches of his glory in Christ Jesus." When I act upon Psalm 4:8, "I will both lie down in peace, and sleep; for You alone, O Lord, make me dwell in safety" (NKJV), I discover I can trust God to watch over me.

When God filled His Word with promises, He had much more in mind than handing us a wish list and turning us loose. In every book of the Bible, He tucked glimpses of His divine nature, guidance to help us navigate life, and opportunities to grow in our faith. Best of all, He gave us sure and certain reasons to pray with confidence. Unlike Dad, who probably wasn't too eager to race me around the apartment, God doesn't have to be coaxed or cajoled to keep His word. "He who promised is faithful," Hebrews 10:23 assures us. Knowing this, we can pray God's promises with confidence and trust.

Uncommon Power

God's promises not only reveal His divine nature, lead us in paths of righteousness, and mature our faith; they encourage us to pray boldly for what God has promised.

Praise Prompt

Father, thank you for filling your Word with promises. Because you never make a promise you don't intend to keep, I have your permission to pray confidently. Like a trusting child in the care of a faithful father, help me grow my love and faith. In the strong name of Jesus I ask, amen.

Live It Out

The next time you encounter one of God's promises, ask yourself: What is the purpose of this promise? Is it to reveal something about God's character? Provide guidance for my life? Or invite me to take God at His word and trust Him? Whatever He's doing, respond in faith, confidence, and trust.

33

Every Promise in the Book Isn't Mine

The promise is for you and your children and for all who are far off—for all whom the Lord our God will call.

ACTS 2:39

When I graduated from high school, a sweet lady from church gave me a book of Bible promises. The slender volume contained hundreds of verses plucked from the pages of Scripture. As I leafed through the book, I felt like the sorcerer's apprentice when he came upon the wizard's book of magic spells. If I could find the right promise and claim it, then I could have whatever I wanted, right?

In the years since, I've learned, contrary to what the children's chorus says, every promise in the Book isn't mine.

But many of them are. How can we know which are and which aren't?

A helpful rule of thumb is to ask three questions:

1. To whom is the promise given? (An individual? A group? Christians? Everyone?)

2. What is the context of the promise? (Read the surrounding verses. What is happening?)

3. Is the promise conditional or unconditional? (Do I have to do something to receive the promise, or does it all depend on God?)

Take for example God's promise to give Abram a son through his wife, Sarai. If we ignore the context of the verse, someone struggling to conceive might be tempted to lift it from the pages of Genesis and claim it as her own: "I will bless her and will surely give you a son by her" (Genesis 17:16). But if we read the passage in its entirety, we see this is a one-time promise from God to Abram.

We also realize the promise is unconditional. Its fulfillment depends entirely on God. We know this because the rest of the story shows how Abram questioned God's ability and Sarai laughed out loud at the thought of a ninety-year-old woman conceiving a child. No doubt about it; God did it all.

In contrast, consider the conditional promises of Deuteronomy 28:1–14. God told the Israelites He would grant them superiority over the other nations; give them successful cities and farming; children, food, and livestock; abundant rain; and protection against enemies and disease. These promises, however, came with one *big* condition: "*If* you fully obey the LORD your God and carefully follow all his commands I give you today" (v. 1).

To differentiate between conditional and unconditional promises, look for the telltale word *if.*

Many of the promises (conditional and unconditional) God gave Old Testament believers apply to us as well, because we've been grafted into the spiritual family tree of Israel.

He gives Christians conditional promises:

> Know therefore that the LORD your God is God; he is the faithful God, keeping his covenant of love to a thousand generations of *those who love him and keep his commandments.* (Deuteronomy 7:9)

> *If* my people, who are called by my name, will humble themselves and pray and seek my face and turn from their wicked ways, *then* I will hear from heaven, and I will forgive their sin and will heal their land. (2 Chronicles 7:14)

And He gives us unconditional promises:

> For the wages of sin is death, but the gift of God is eternal life in Christ Jesus our Lord. (Romans 6:23)

> No temptation has overtaken you except what is common to mankind. And God is faithful; he will not let you be tempted beyond what you can bear. But when you are tempted, he will also provide a way out so that you can endure it. (1 Corinthians 10:13)

Is every promise in the Book mine? No.

But a lot of them are.

As we prayerfully and carefully study God's Word, we can trust Him to show us which ones. This process helps us refine and direct our prayers. It protects us from disappointment and ensures we'll pray efficiently and according to God's will.

Uncommon Power

When I carefully discern which promises in the Bible are for me, I can know what to pray for in faith and with expectation, because God is always faithful to His promises.

Praise Prompt

Father, thank you for being a faithful God who loves to bless and care for your people. You have filled your Word with promises for provision, protection, and blessing. Help us stand confidently on the promises you've given us. Grant us wisdom to know which belong to us and which do not. Thank you for being a promise-making, promise-keeping Father. In the name of the Lord Jesus Christ I pray, amen.

Live It Out

Each time you encounter a promise in the Bible, ask the three diagnostic questions. Invite the Holy Spirit to teach you how to correctly handle and pray the precious promises of God.

34

The Revealing Power of Prayer

Who can discern their own errors?
Forgive my hidden faults.

PSALM 19:12

As a child, I enjoyed going to the dentist—except for the brushing evaluation. When the dental hygienist handed me the red disclosing tablets, I knew I was probably in trouble. There was no hiding my brushing flaws once those tablets hit my teeth.

"Chew them thoroughly," she said, "then swish and spit."

When I did, every spot I'd missed glowed like Rudolph's nose. The red smudges revealed my toothbrushing transgressions and displayed them for the world to see. The only thing redder than my teeth was my face.

If you'd asked me if I'd brushed well, I'd have boasted yes. But disclosing tablets don't lie.

Neither does God's Word.

Objective and truthful, it searches our hearts and minds for undisclosed sins and exposes them. King David knew this. He wasn't reluctant about exposure, as I was with the chew and swish in the dental chair; he welcomed God's insight into his heart. He knew there were unclean corners and hidden sins that needed to be revealed.

"Who can discern their own errors?" he prayed in Psalm 19:12. "Forgive my hidden faults."

"The heart," Jeremiah 17:9 declares, "is deceitful above all things and beyond cure. Who can understand it?" Just as I believed my childhood toothbrushing efforts were effective, I often think I'm sin-free. The opposite is usually true. Weak faith, a faulty view of God, or deep-rooted selfishness, laziness, or bitterness stain my character like cavity-causing plaque, eating holes in my soul and harming myself and others. If I open my heart to God and invite Him to reveal the sin that lurks inside, He goes to work.

One morning, after I'd asked God to examine my soul, I sat quietly, waiting for His response. It wasn't long before He brought to mind the harsh words I'd spoken to one of my children. Then I remembered how I'd selfishly ignored my husband's needs as I focused on my own. Some days God discloses my sin through a passage I read in the Bible, a message I hear on the radio, or my pastor's sermon.

Sometimes God uses godly friends and mentors to point out my sin. God used Nathan the prophet to confront David about his sins of adultery and murder and begin his journey of repentance and restoration.

Many times when I invite God to show me my sin, then sit quietly and listen, He answers my prayer. Sometimes I realize my disobedience immediately. Other times I gradually become aware of a sinful thought or action that doesn't honor Him. Because I want Him to cleanse my heart and make me more like Jesus, I acknowledge my faults, repent, and ask for His help to change.

Like the gritty polish the hygienist smears on my teeth, time in prayer and God's Word cleanses me. Little by little, my loving Father smooths the rough edges of my character and polishes my thoughts and behaviors. Before long, they shine like a squeaky-clean smile.

Although I dreaded using the disclosing tablets as a kid, I learned to be thankful for how they pointed out the areas I'd missed so I could correct my brushing. Similarly, we can be thankful God's Word and prayer have the power to disclose sin. They help us live clean lives before God and others.

Uncommon Power

God has the power to disclose sins we aren't even aware of. Thankfully, He doesn't just point out the areas of our lives that need cleansing; He forgives us when we ask and empowers us to change.

Praise Prompt

I praise you, precious Father, that you don't allow me to stay in my sin. You promise to complete the good work you began in me at salvation. Whenever you reveal sin in my life, it's because you love me and want me to enjoy the benefits of pure living and a clear conscience. Thank you for your Word, godly friends, and the Holy Spirit inside me to point out where I've gone astray. Thank you for the resurrection power you've placed within me that enables me to triumph over my sin and live a life that honors and glorifies you.

Live It Out

This week, pray Psalm 19:12 at the beginning of your prayer and Bible reading times. Ask God to examine your heart and reveal any sin. Write down what He shows you through His Word, other believers, and the quiet voice of the Holy Spirit. Confess and forsake it. Invite Him to change you to be more like Jesus.

35

If Jesus Paid for My Sins, Why Must I Confess?

**If we confess our sins, he is faithful and just
and will forgive us our sins and purify us
from all unrighteousness.**

1 JOHN 1:9

No parent ever wants to hear their child's hysterical voice on the other end of the phone line. At first, all I could distinguish was the occasional word punctuated by frightened sobs. "Thrill Hill . . . accident . . . totaled . . . police."

As I struggled to make sense of what my daughter was trying to communicate, I thanked God that she was, apparently, still alive. No one on the verge of death could make that much noise. I asked questions, trying to figure out what happened.

"Are you hurt?"

"Are your friends hurt?"

"Where are you?"

"We'll be right there."

When my husband and I arrived at the scene, we wrapped our arms around our frightened daughter and hugged her—hard. Then we sorted out the details.

Driving too fast and showing off to her carload of friends, Mary Leigh had crested the hill. A car was stopped in the middle of the street, hidden by the slope of the road. She plowed into it, injuring the driver, and totaling both cars. Mercifully, the driver suffered only a broken arm, and no one in her car was hurt.

Car insurance covered the damages and paid the driver's hospital bills. Mary Leigh was cited and paid the penalty for her poor choices—a mild concussion and a wrecked car.

"I was driving too fast," she confessed to us after the accident. "I know you trusted me, and I didn't act very responsibly. I'm so sorry."

I shared this story when a new believer asked, "If Jesus's death on the cross paid the penalty for my sin, why do I need to confess it and ask God to forgive me? Aren't I already forgiven?"

Yes, we are forgiven. First John 1:9 tells us clearly: "If we confess our sins, he is faithful and just and will forgive us our sins and purify us from all unrighteousness." This verse provides the prescription for cleansing, purity, and spiritual growth.

When Christ died on the cross, He satisfied the sin debt of all who would believe in Him. When we accept by faith what He did on our behalf, God removes the punishment from our account. Like a criminal condemned to die in the electric chair who receives a pardon, we've been spared the eternal punishment for our actions.

But the Christian life isn't just about avoiding the punishment our sins deserve. It isn't only about a one-time need for forgiveness.

God calls us to confess our sins so we can experience the fullness of the freedom He bought for us. He desires for us to have clean hearts, surrendered lives, close relationships with Him, and unhindered prayers. Confessional prayer demonstrates we agree with God that what we've done is wrong and that we are no longer slaves to sin. It frees us to accept the forgiveness He offers and receive the cleansing He promises. If we confess our sins in prayer as soon as we become aware of them, we can enjoy the fruitfulness and freedom God intends for His children to have.

When our daughter drove recklessly, she broke the law and disregarded the rules we had put in place to protect and bless her. The insurance company replaced the totaled car, but her admission of guilt and sincere apology enabled her to once again live in the freedom and protection of our guidance.

Uncommon Power

Prayers of confession break the power of sin in our lives and enable us to walk in freedom.

Praise Prompt

Heavenly Father, thank you for sending Jesus to remove forever the penalty for my sin. What a joy to have an unhindered relationship with you. I love being your child. Thank you for forgiving my sin every time I confess it. Help me never to take lightly your willingness to forgive. Remind me that you've given me the power to say no to those sins that tempt me. Help me walk in the freedom you purchased for me on the cross. In Jesus's precious name I pray, amen.

Live It Out

The next time you become aware of your sin, confess it immediately. Demonstrate that you've accepted God's forgiveness by refusing to condemn yourself for your failures. Cooperate with God as He cleanses you from all unrighteousness and makes you more like His Son.

36

Lead Us Not into Temptation

Lead us not into temptation,
but deliver us from the evil one.

MATTHEW 6:13

We will struggle with sin until we die or until Jesus comes to take us home. Although Christ defeated the power of sin on the cross, the battle still rages in our earthly bodies. Our spiritual nature is perfect, but our flesh remains under construction.

Like the apostle Paul, who lamented in Romans 7:19 and 24 about his struggle with the flesh, we cry out, "I do not do the good I want to do, but the evil I do not want to do—this I keep on doing . . . What a wretched man I am! Who will rescue me from this body that is subject to death?"

This reality explains why Jesus, in His model prayer, taught His disciples to pray, "Lead us not into temptation, but deliver us from the evil one" (Matthew 6:13). He knew Satan has filled our world with spiritual landmines and only supernatural help can enable us to successfully navigate the battlefield.

James 1:13 makes it clear God never tempts us to do evil. To do so would go against His desire for us to be holy as He is holy (1 Peter 1:16). But God does allow temptation and trials into our lives to prove and grow our faith. Job's trials and Jesus's own temptation in the wilderness provide examples of this.

Yet in this twelve-word line from Jesus's model prayer, God gives us permission to ask Him to spare us from trials and shield us from temptation.

When we do, we accomplish several things.

First, we acknowledge our flesh is weak, that it struggles to do the right thing. Although our spirit wants to say kind words, do good deeds, and honor God in everything we do, we often fail. We tear down instead of build up and complain instead of express our thanks. We consume the junk food of today's media instead of feasting on the pure nutrition of God's Word. We waste our time, money, and effort on temporary things and fail to invest in God's kingdom. We sin against God, ourselves, and others. When we ask God to steer us away from these temptations, we admit to Him (and to ourselves) that we need His help.

Second, when we encounter a temptation or trial after asking God to steer us away from it, we know He's allowed the test to give us an opportunity to succeed. First Corinthians 10:13 assures us, God "will not let you be tempted beyond what you can bear. But when you are tempted, he will also provide a way out so that you can endure it." Seeing the test for what it is—an opportunity to glorify God— enables us to look for the way of escape and take it.

Finally, praying for God to direct us away from trials and temptations reminds us we can trust His sovereignty over the events of our lives. It's not wrong to want to be spared from trials, suffering, and temptation if we submit ourselves to God's will, whatever the outcome.

Several years ago, I was challenged by James 4:2, "You do not have because you do not ask God." After watching several friends struggle with and lose their battles with cancer, and witnessing others experience the excruciating trial of caring for a loved one with Alzheimer's, I began to ask God daily to protect our family from these two diseases.

I don't know if God will answer this prayer. It may be His will for us to experience these trials so He can grow our faith and glorify Him through our suffering. But I'd prefer not to experience them if this is His will for me.

The same is true with temptation. We can glorify God by resisting an acquaintance's flirtatious advances, but how much better would it be if God steered us completely away from such an encounter? I often ask God to protect my husband and sons-in-law from the temptations of lust and pornography and give them strength to resist if the opportunity comes their way.

I like to pray this version of Jesus's model prayer: "Lord, if it is your will, spare me from trial and temptation. But if you choose to allow it into my life, give me the strength to endure it and the ability to glorify you through it."

Uncommon Power

When we pray daily for God to steer us away from temptation, we tap into a powerful means of protection.

Praise Prompt

I praise you, Lord, for having control over everything that enters my life. I don't have to fear trial or temptation because you, not Satan, are the gatekeeper. I praise you that "the one who is in [me] is greater than the one who is in the world" (1 John 4:4). I will not be afraid, knowing that everything you allow into my life is filtered through your hands of love. Help me glorify you in trial and in triumph and call upon you when I'm tempted.

Live It Out

If you haven't developed the practice of asking God to deliver you and those you love from temptation and trial, begin now. If you're struggling with a particular temptation, call it by name as you ask God to lead you away from that specific sin. If you're experiencing a trial, ask Him for strength to glorify Him in the midst of it.

37

Pray Like a Cheetah

The lions roar for their prey,
and seek their food from God.

PSALM 104:21

My granddaughters are fascinated with all things nature, so one morning we read a *National Geographic* book about wildcats.

"And then the cheetah sneaks up on his prey and pounces," I read.

"But, Gigi," three-year-old Caroline said, "how do cheetahs pray? Like this? 'Dear Jesus, please help me catch that antelope.'"

As we burst into giggles at the mental picture she described, I wondered how in the world I could explain to a preschooler that *prey* and *pray* are homophones—words that sound the same but have different meanings.

I decided to ride the wave of laughter and save the grammar lesson for another day.

"Maybe they pray, 'Dear God, please send me two rabbits, a coyote, and a beaver. And two mice for dessert,'" I said. They laughed again, picturing a cheetah on its knees praying for its dinner.

When their laughter subsided, I introduced a new thought, "You know, animals don't have to pray for their food. The Bible says, 'The lions roar for their prey, and seek their food from God' (Psalm 104:21). God feeds them. He feeds the birds too. And best of all, He feeds us."

Moments like these give me a chance to share truths about God with my grandchildren. They also remind me of what I occasionally forget. Matthew 6:8 says, "Your Father knows what you need before you ask him."

This doesn't mean I shouldn't pray about my needs. It means that once I have prayed, I can leave my requests in God's hands, confident He will provide. I don't have to beg, petition, build a case, or defend my request. God calls me simply to ask, like a child coming to a benevolent parent when she's hungry. Or a cheetah asking for an antelope.

Sometimes I forget God is eager to meet my needs. Matthew 7:9–11 poses a question that spotlights how ludicrous it is to ask God to provide and then doubt He will: "Which of you, if your son asks for bread, will give him a stone? Or if he asks for a fish, will give him a snake? If you, then, though you are evil, know how to give good gifts to your children, how much more will your Father in heaven give good gifts to those who ask him!"

How silly of me to doubt!

I pray and fret, and pray and worry, and pray and cajole. What an inaccurate picture I paint for the watching world: a daughter with a legitimate need approaching her loving Father as if He were a deadbeat dad.

As the girls and I continued to read, we turned to a two-page spread of the cheetah standing proudly over the prone body of a large animal.

"Look, Caroline," I said, "the cheetah caught a great big antelope for dinner."

"Wow, Gigi," she replied, "God musta known he was reeeeeeally hungry."

Uncommon Power

Since God has promised to meet my needs, I can pray from a place of rest, secure in His provision.

Praise Prompt

Father, forgive me for the times I doubt you. For the times I fail to trust your character. You don't deserve my skepticism. You've met my needs all the days of my life, through sickness, job loss, and financial challenge. Teach me to ask for what I need with confidence, knowing your generous and gracious heart will provide everything, in your timing, according to your riches, and for your glory. In the strong name of Jesus I ask, amen.

Live It Out

Think about your basic needs: food, clothing, medicine, and somewhere to live. Have you ever felt anxious or fearful, wondering if God will meet your needs? Have you prayed about it? When you pray, do you pray with bold confidence or trembling uncertainty? Resolve today to approach God as a beloved child, not a hesitant stranger. Ask Him to meet your needs, then trust that He will.

38

Big Needs and
Small Ones

Until now you have not asked for anything
in my name. Ask and you will receive, and
your joy will be complete.

JOHN 16:24

I went from spiritual to sheepish with six words from Sister Freda Robinson: "Please pray for food and medicine."

I've known of Sister Freda for years through friends. A soft-spoken, regal Kenyan, she's a woman with big dreams—dreams that are coming true.

Since 2004, when she left her job as a nurse, she's served the poorest and sickest citizens of Kitale, Kenya. She's founded a hospital, an outreach clinic, a preschool, a feeding program, a girls' school, and a nursing college.

When my friend Debbie, who's taken several mission trips to work in Sister Freda's hospital, got married, Sister Freda travelled from Kenya to be her maid of honor.

Freda and I sat together at the reception. She told me about her ministry, and I told her about my book project, *Refresh Your Faith: Uncommon Devotions from Every Book of the Bible.* "I want to help women get excited about God's Word," I said. "I believe the Lord has called me to write a devotional spotlighting uncommon and unusual verses in the Bible."

Because I knew she was a powerful prayer warrior, I asked her to pray my book would find favor with a publisher. Then I asked how I could pray for her. Her response made my heart hurt.

"Please pray for food and medicine. And we're trying to build another building. The rainy season is beginning, and we can't feed the children outside in the rain."

That's when I felt small—asking her to pray for my book project when she was trying to feed children and save lives.

Have you ever felt ashamed to share your "little" prayer requests in light of "big" ones? I mean, what's a devotional book compared to hungry children and sick Kenyans?

What's a better job compared to cancer? Or a tight budget compared to a family member addicted to cocaine? Or the loss of a pet compared to the loss of a spouse?

Is it right to pray (or ask for prayer) for our own small needs when others are facing life-threatening, earth-shattering events?

After much wrestling and soul-searching, I can confidently say it is right. And good. And encouraged by God.

Here's why:

1. God hears all our prayers.

"Surely the arm of the Lord is not too short to save, nor his ear too dull to hear," Isaiah 59:1 assures us. My "small" prayers don't prevent God from hearing Sister Freda's "big" prayers.

When my children were young, I often said, "I may have two ears, but I only have one brain. Talk to me one at a time." Thankfully, God isn't limited by human frailties. He hears the cries of all His children and responds even before we say "Amen." "Before they call I will answer," He promises; "while they are still speaking I will hear" (Isaiah 65:24).

2. All our requests are equal in light of God's power.

Unlike us, God doesn't rank needs on a scale of difficulty. Curing cancer is just as easy for Him as providing money for schoolbooks. His power is beyond measure and He specializes in miracles.

"Is anything too hard for the LORD?" God asked Abraham when Abraham laughed at the promise that his ninety-year-old wife would have a child (Genesis 18:14). This same truth levels the playing field for our prayer requests.

3. God's resources aren't limited.

I remember as a teenager asking my mom for a pair of jeans. "I can't buy them this month," she said. "Your sister needs a winter coat." Money was limited in our one-income family, so she had to prioritize our family's needs. The greater need got the yes. The lesser need had to wait.

In God's economy there are enough resources for every need. I don't have to worry that a child will go without clothing in Venezuela if I ask God for money to buy my husband a birthday present.

4. God calls us to different ministries and cares about each one's success.

Sister Freda's calling to save lives, feed orphans, and train women is remarkable. Equally remarkable (although I don't always feel this way) is my calling to write. Because God uses both our callings to point people to himself, one ministry isn't more important than the other. They both have a part in God's great plan.

Since that heart-baring conversation at my friend Debbie's wedding, it's been my privilege to pray for food and medicine for Sister Freda's ministry. I'm confident she feels equally committed to pray for my writing. Together we're doing our best to fulfill the calling God has placed upon our lives. As we pray for each other, we partner with God to accomplish His will and work in the world.

And that's nothing to feel ashamed about.

Uncommon Power

God encourages us to bring all our needs, big and small, to Him in prayer.

Praise Prompt

Oh, Father! How marvelous is your mind and your heart. They are big enough not only to hear the prayers of your children, but to answer them. Because your power is limitless, I can bring every need and concern—big, small, and everywhere in between—to you with confidence. Nothing is too great for you to handle, and nothing is too small for you to consider insignificant. Help me never feel ashamed to bring my "little" needs to you.

Live It Out

Examine your prayer life. Do you tend to limit your prayer requests to "big" needs only? Today, commit to bring all your needs to the Father, then watch to see how He answers.

39

Who Are You Listening To?

**And he said, "Who told you
that you were naked?"**

GENESIS 3:11

Do you remember the legend about George Washington and the cherry tree? In the original version, which appeared in Mason Locke Weems's biography, *The Life of Washington*, six-year-old George received a hatchet as a gift. He couldn't resist trying it out—on his father's cherry tree. When his father discovered the damage to the tree, he became angry and confronted him.

"George, do you know who killed that beautiful little cherry-tree?"

"I can't tell a lie," young George supposedly said. "I did cut it with my hatchet."

Washington's father commended him for telling the truth, saying that his son's honesty was worth more than a thousand trees.[11]

Long before George Washington came along, God asked Adam a father-son question that also involved sin and a tree.

"Where are you?" (Genesis 3:9).

Like Mr. Washington, God didn't ask the question to obtain information. Both fathers knew the truth. Just as the ax blade perfectly matched the cut in Washington's tree, so did Adam's incisors fit perfectly into the bite mark in Eve's fruit.

God (and Mr. Washington) asked questions to give their sons a chance to admit their sin and come clean. To tell the truth, confess, repent, and be restored.

George chose honesty. Adam did not. "I heard you in the garden," Adam said, "and I was afraid because I was naked; so I hid" (v. 10).

God then asked a second question: "Who told you that you were naked? Have you eaten from the tree that I commanded you not to eat from?" (v. 11). In other words, "When you were tempted to sin, who were you listening to?"

Adam's answer—"the woman you put here with me"—and Eve's answer—"the serpent"—revealed the root cause of every sin that enters our life. We sin whenever we listen to anything and anyone but God. When we dismiss God's Word and listen to the world, the culture, our feelings, popular opinion, our friends' advice, or, as in Adam and Eve's case, Satan himself, we take the first step on sin's slippery path.

The voices in our heads whisper that we're worthless, the situation's hopeless, and nothing will ever change. The education system tells us God is a myth, man is just a higher animal, and our productivity determines our worth. Our culture whispers that unborn babies are disposable, our actions impact only ourselves, and we should follow our hearts.

Prayer (us talking to God) and Bible reading (God talking to us), on the other hand, fills our minds with God's truth and filters out the enemy's lies. James 1:5 promises, "If any of you lacks wisdom, you should ask God, who gives generously to all without finding fault, and it will be given to you."

The next time you wrestle with a decision, struggle with a besetting sin, or languish because of an unfulfilled longing, remember God's second question to Adam—"Who told you that?"—and pray for discernment.

If the answer you receive is anyone or anything that's not based on God and His Word, run the other way. The voice of God's truth, discerned through Bible reading, prayer, and godly counsel is the only voice we can trust completely.

Uncommon Power

Prayer (talking to God) and reading God's Word (God talking to me) helps me access the discernment I need to avoid sin and live a godly life.

Praise Prompt

I praise you, God, for filling your Word with wisdom and making it readily available. You've provided everything I need. With the Bible as my guide, I can navigate life confidently, because your Word will never lead me astray. Thank you for making your wisdom available to me every day. In humble gratitude I pray, amen.

Live It Out

The next time you feel confused, depressed, condemned, or tempted, ask yourself, "Whose voice am I listening to? Who told me that?" Ask God to give you a spirit of discernment to discover who or what is influencing you.

40

More than Healing

**This happened so that the works of God
might be displayed in him.**

JOHN 9:3

My friend Catherine and I were sharing lunch together at a tiny café that served the best pimento cheese in town. After catching up on family news, our conversation turned to matters of faith.

"When I was first diagnosed," she confided, "I prayed for healing every single day."

"I can understand that," I said. "I would too."

"After a while though, something changed." She stretched the paper straw wrapper flat on the table in front of her and raised her eyes to meet mine. "I still ask God to take away my disease sometimes, but now I pray for so much more."

Catherine has been on my prayer list since she first got sick. I often ask God to heal her and make her life pain-free. As I watch her navigate the ups and downs of chronic illness, she's taught me there's much more to praying for the sick than asking God to heal them.

The apostle Paul suffered from a chronic condition many scholars believe was a painful eye ailment.[12] Whatever it was forced him to rely on others and hindered him from doing many things he wanted to do. Unlike some who have romanticized their sickness, Paul called it a "thorn in my flesh" and "a messenger of Satan" (2 Corinthians 12:7). He pleaded with God three times to remove it, and three times, God said no (v. 8).

If you're like me, the first thing you do when someone you care about gets sick is to ask God to heal them. This is biblical. James 5:14 tells us, "Is anyone among you sick? Let them call the elders of the church to pray over them and anoint them with oil in the name of the Lord." Oftentimes, James observed, "the prayer offered in faith will make the sick person well; the Lord will raise them up" (v. 15).

But not always.

Such was the case with Paul. Such is the case with many we love.

Sometimes, despite thousands of prayers offered in sincere faith by godly believers, God chooses not to heal. With our limited understanding, this is difficult to accept, but we can trust that God has an eternal purpose for everything He allows.

If you know someone who's sick, in addition to asking God to heal them, consider adding these requests to your prayers:

1. Pray for them to come to faith in Christ or grow in their faith.

I believe God has one of two reasons for every circumstance He allows into a person's life. If they don't know Christ as Savior, God orchestrates the details of their lives to point them to himself. We must never forget that our sick, unbelieving friend's greatest need isn't physical healing. It's spiritual healing.

If a person does have a relationship with Christ, we know God allows every trial that enters their life to make them more like Jesus (Romans 8:29).

2. Pray God will be glorified through their illness.

When Jesus encountered a man born blind, His disciples asked Him, "Rabbi, who sinned, this man or his parents, that he was born blind?" (John 9:2).

"Neither this man nor his parents sinned," Jesus said, "but this happened so that the works of God might be displayed in him" (v. 3). When we pray for those suffering from physical and emotional ailments, we can ask God to glorify himself in and through their lives. We can pray God will give our sick friends ample opportunities to testify of His goodness, even in the midst of their suffering. When believers walk the path of illness with faith and confidence in God's steadfast love, they accurately represent our good God and glorify Him.

3. Pray for God to supply strength, grace, and provision.

When God said no to Paul's plea for healing, He revealed one of the reasons He allows physical and emotional weakness. "My grace is sufficient for you, for my power is made perfect in weakness" (2 Corinthians 12:9).

"Therefore," Paul responded, "I will boast all the more gladly about my weaknesses, so that Christ's power may rest on me. That is why, for Christ's sake, I delight in weaknesses, in insults, in hardships, in persecutions, in difficulties. For when I am weak, then I am strong" (vv. 9–10).

Similarly, we can pray that our loved ones will rely on God's strength, not their own, during times of weakness. We can ask God to supply their needs according to the riches of His glory (Philippians 4:19) and give them grace to face each day with faith and trust.

4. Pray for others to be drawn to Christ through your loved one's suffering.

Unbelievers expect Christians to praise God when their health is good, their fortunes are secure, and their families are prospering. Even Satan, commenting on Job's godly lifestyle, said, "Does Job fear God for nothing? . . . Have you not put a hedge around him and his household and everything he has? . . . But now stretch out your hand and strike everything he has," Satan challenged, "and he will surely curse you to your face" (Job 1:9–11).

The unbelieving world takes notice of a Christian in the throes of suffering. It watches to see if their faith will stand firm and their hope remain secure. People who are searching want to see God provide everything a Christian needs to weather the storm of physical or emotional illness. They're drawn toward God when a wounded believer loses all the observable reasons for following God yet remains firm in their faith.

God's Word reminds us to pray for those who are sick. He invites us to ask Him to heal them. Beyond that, we can ask God to glorify himself, meet their needs, grow their faith, and draw others to God through their illness. When we do, we come alongside Him as He redeems their suffering and uses it for His good purposes.

Uncommon Power

We can pray for physical healing and so much more for those we love.

Praise Prompt

Father, it's easy to grow discouraged at the number of sick and hurting people around me. But you never intended for your creation to suffer sickness and death. Sin did that. And for a time, you have allowed it. What a comfort to know that you are intimately aware of all our needs and are attuned to our suffering. Thank you that you are not cruel or uncaring. I praise you that one day soon we'll join you in a forever world with no sickness, pain, or death. Until that day, help me trust that you won't waste a moment of the suffering your children experience. Use it to draw many into a saving relationship with your Son, and conform us all to your image. In the strong name of Jesus I ask, amen.

Live It Out

Today, as you pray for the sick on your prayer list, ask God to show you their needs beyond physical healing. Consider the thought that perhaps God is allowing their illness to accomplish something greater than just restoring their health. Pray as God leads you for their spiritual well-being, testimony to the world around them, and impact on the lost.

41

Raising Lazarus (and Wormi)

But as for me, I watch in hope for the
LORD, I wait for God my Savior;
my God will hear me.

MICAH 7:7

My first sincere prayer raised the dead.

Subsequent prayers have produced less dramatic results.

I was sixteen years old, not a drama queen by any stretch of the imagination, but every bit a teenage girl. My highs were Pikes Peak, and my lows were the soil at the base of the Grand Canyon.

I'd been attending a church that taught that God hears and answers prayers. I learned He was powerful, compassionate, and loving.

One night these truths became especially meaningful to me—the night Wormi died.

Wormi was my favorite fish. A kuhli loach, Wormi looked like a brown ribbon with eyes and whiskers. His eellike body sported orange stripes and a tail that could propel him through the water at exceptional speed. He'd zoom around the tank, delighting my sisters and me with his antics. The tank had a lid, just in case he launched himself out of the water and tried to fly.

Every night before I climbed into bed, I counted my fish. Six months earlier the pimelodella catfish had scarfed up a tiger barb, and I'd begun doing roll call at bedtime. That night, all were accounted for except Wormi.

Most days he'd drape himself in one of the plastic trees that lined the back of the aquarium, slither into the fake castle, or camouflage among the coral, but that night, I didn't see him anywhere.

Then I noticed the cover to the aquarium was askew. My stomach clenched as I scanned the carpet in front of the tank. There, in the center of a ball of carpet fuzz, was Wormi, curled into a perfect U and crispy as an autumn leaf.

My scream brought every member of the family running. I scooped him up, fuzz and all, and plopped him into the tank. I watched in horror as he and his fuzzy sweater sank to the bottom, where he rested, lifeless and stiff.

No amount of consoling could quiet my brokenhearted wails. Mom offered to buy me a new fish. My sisters hugged and patted me. Dad stood by in silent solidarity, helpless to ease my pain.

When time passed and Wormi showed no signs of life, I turned out the light and crawled into bed sobbing. That's when I remembered prayer.

"Lord," I whispered as fresh tears wet my cheeks, "you raised Lazarus from the dead. Couldn't you raise Wormi too? I know he's just a fish, but he's my favorite fish. I love him." I thought about how the pious ladies in church prayed and added, "In Jesus's name I pray, amen."

I switched on the light to see if God had answered my prayer, but Wormi remained curved like a horseshoe in the ball of carpet fuzz. *I'll bury him in the morning*, I thought and turned out the light.

I slept fitfully and awakened with a heavy heart. Knowing I couldn't postpone the inevitable, I grabbed the net.

Eying the hairy glob of fuzz at the bottom of the tank, I blinked. And blinked again. The wad of carpet fiber hadn't moved, but Wormi was gone.

God took him to heaven, I thought in surprise.

Then a movement caught my eye. There, in the corner of the aquarium, draped in his favorite tree, sat Wormi. Bright-eyed and whiskery, he looked no worse for his experience. I screamed, again drawing my family from all parts of the house.

"God heard my prayer. God heard my prayer. He raised Wormi from the dead!" Tears streamed down my face as my sisters joined me in a happy dance that would have made Snoopy proud.

I've grown a lot since that first heartbroken prayer. I've learned it's not always God's will to heal and restore. But sometimes it is.

Wormi's resurrection day marks a crucial point in my spiritual life. It fixed forever in my heart the truth that God hears and responds to our prayers. That night, I believe He wanted to encourage my fledgling faith by performing a small (but huge to me) miracle. He wanted to teach me to call to Him for help and to learn to "watch in hope for the LORD," knowing that "my God will hear me" (Micah 7:7).

Because of Wormi, I know I pray to a God who has the power to do miracles. The more I pray and watch how He answers (sometimes yes, and sometimes no), the more I learn to trust Him and wait expectantly for the unexpected.

Uncommon Power

We can come to God with impossible prayers because He has the power to do impossible things.

Praise Prompt

Oh, Father, nothing is too hard for you. When I'm tempted not to pray because the situation seems hopeless or the need too great, remind me that you are the God who created the world from nothing, hung the universe in place, and raised the dead to life. I don't have to limit my prayers, because your power is more than enough. Grow my faith. Increase my trust. Use my prayers to bring you glory. In the strong name of Jesus I pray, amen.

Live It Out

If you've been a Christian for very long, you know God doesn't always do miracles in response to our prayers. But sometimes He does. Wouldn't you hate to miss a miracle because you didn't have the faith to ask for it? Commit today never to underestimate or second-guess God. The next time you encounter a situation that can only be fixed by a miracle, ask God for it. Who knows if your prayer might be the catalyst to release God's power into your situation?

42

When We Don't Know What to Pray

In the same way, the Spirit helps us in our
weakness. We do not know what we ought
to pray for, but the Spirit himself intercedes
for us through wordless groans.

ROMANS 8:26

I've always been a wordy person, but on Monday, October 3, 1994, I had no words. The week before, my husband, David, had lost his job. On the day he planned to search for a new job, he awakened to extreme nausea and violent stomach pains. The next day, our car broke down.

His illness continued, preventing him from looking for another job. When we sought medical care, we learned his insurance benefits had ended with his job. Feeling a bit like Job, I gathered our young children close and watched for gale force winds and falling roofs (Job 1:19).

I reached the end of myself that Monday morning.

"Lord," I prayed, "this situation is broken in so many ways I don't even know how to pray. Help us, Father, just help us." I laid my head on the kitchen table and sobbed.

I'm grateful our prayers don't stop when our words run out or our insight fails. In these moments, we have an Advocate, one who prays for us—God the Holy Spirit. "In the same way, the Spirit helps us in our weakness," the apostle Paul wrote. "We do not know what we ought to pray for, but the Spirit himself intercedes for us through wordless groans" (Romans 8:26).

The gift of the Intercessor/Advocate, the *paraclete*, as John called Him, comes from Jesus himself. He promised in John 14:16–17, "I will ask the Father, and he will give you another advocate to help you and be with you forever—the Spirit of truth. The world cannot accept him, because it neither sees him nor knows him. But you know him, for he lives with you and will be in you."

John used the Greek word *paraclete*, which comes from two words: *pará*, which means "close-beside" and *kaléō*, which means "make a call."[13] Together they describe a legal advocate who makes the right judgment call because he is close to the situation.

What a beautiful job description for the third member of the Trinity. God the Holy Spirit walks so closely with us (and lives within us) that He knows every detail of our thoughts, emotions, and needs.

On that day in October when I felt so overwhelmed by the circumstances of my life that I couldn't find words to express my need, God the Holy Spirit spoke for me. Like an attorney advocating for his client, He assessed my needs, articulated my thoughts, and made a plea on my behalf.

Scripture encourages us to pray specifically. It pleases God to hear us claim His promises in faith. But some days, all we can do is cry out to God and rely on the Holy Spirit to do the rest.

Although my family's situation didn't resolve immediately, glimmers of light dawned. A friend helped us with car repairs. Temporary insurance allowed David to seek medical care. Anonymous donations helped us pay our bills. In time David regained his health and found a new job.

God's care and provision for us during that challenging time proved that while I hadn't known what to pray, the Holy Spirit, my Advocate, had.

Uncommon Power

When we don't know what to pray, God the Holy Spirit prays for us.

Praise Prompt

Precious Savior, you knew we couldn't navigate this troubled world on our own, so you sent us an Advocate, the Holy Spirit. He is someone who not only walks beside us but lives within us, never leaving us nor forsaking us. Knowing He will take our cries and our tears and translate them into petitions on our behalf comforts us in our deepest times of distress. Thank you, Lord Jesus, for the gift of the Holy Spirit.

Live It Out

Is there a situation in your life that seems so messed up you don't even know how to ask God to fix it? Take heart. You don't have to figure it out. The Holy Spirit knows what you need. Cry out to Him, and He will carry your requests to God the Father.

43

How to Seek God's Will

As for me, the LORD has
led me on the journey.

GENESIS 24:27

I've always envied the people who could gather information, assess a situation, and make a decision fairly quickly. Not me. When presented with a choice, I struggle. As a youngster, while all the other kids stepped confidently up to Jimmy the Ice Cream Man's white truck and placed their orders, I vacillated. Maple walnut ice cream or raspberry sherbet? I loved them both.

As I grew older, the choices grew more complicated, and the ramifications of my decisions weighed heavier. I suspect you've experienced similar angst.

I wish I had read Genesis 24 much sooner. I could have learned from Eliezer,[14] the servant of Abraham, and avoided a host of sleepless nights.

Abraham lived in Canaan, the land God had promised to give him and his descendants. He had two sons and one plot of land— the burial site of his wife, Sarah. But God had promised to create through Abraham a nation of people to follow the Lord. When the time came for Isaac, Abraham's sole heir, to take a wife, Abraham knew he couldn't marry a pagan Canaanite. He had to marry kin. (It was okay in those days. The gene pool hadn't yet become corrupted.)

So he dispatched his trusted servant, Eliezer, to find a wife for Isaac from among his family in Mesopotamia.

Eliezer had grown up in Abraham's home. He had watched his master make wise (and not-so-wise) decisions during his hundred years of walking with God. He knew what to do.

We can draw six principles for decision-making from Eliezer's example.

1. Follow the revealed will of your master. Abraham gave specific instructions: "You will not get a wife for my son from the daughters of the Canaanites . . . but you will go to my country and my own relatives and get a wife for my son Isaac" (vv. 3–4). When we face similarly significant life decisions, we don't always have such specific instructions from God, our Master, but we do have the general wisdom of the Bible. It's wise, then, to follow the commands and principles given in His Word.

2. Invite God into the search. Eliezer asked God for favor and direction: "LORD, God of my master Abraham, make me successful today, and show kindness to my master Abraham" (v. 12). This point seems simplistic, but we often forget it. We consult friends and advisers, but we fail to ask the all-wise Counselor to bless and guide our decision.

3. Pray specifically. Eliezer didn't ask for some pretty girl to cross his path to bring home to Isaac. Instead, he looked up, saw the young women of the city coming to draw water from the well, and asked God for specific direction. "May it be that when I say to a young woman, 'Please let down your jar that I may have a drink,' and she says, 'Drink, and I'll water your camels too'—let her be the one you have chosen for your servant Isaac. By this I will know that you have shown kindness to my master" (v. 14).

And what do you know? "Before he had finished praying, Rebekah came out with her jar on her shoulder. She was the daughter of Bethuel son of Milkah, who was the wife of Abraham's brother Nahor" (v. 15).

4. Worship God when He answers your prayer. When Eliezer realized God had answered his prayer and Rebekah was the one, he bowed in holy awe. "Praise be to the LORD, the God of my master Abraham, who has not abandoned his kindness and faithfulness to my master. As for me, the LORD has led me on the journey to the house of my master's relatives" (vv. 26–27).

5. Tell others how God has guided you. Sharing faith stories with others strengthens their faith and helps them trust God too. When Eliezer described the details of his quest to Rebekah and her family and how God had specifically answered his prayers, they couldn't doubt that the circumstances were from God. They surrendered eagerly and wholeheartedly to God's will (vv. 50–51).

6. Watch how God uses your obedience in far-reaching ways. Eliezer's assignment was to find a wife for his master's son, Isaac. We know Isaac married Rebekah, who bore Jacob and Esau. Jacob had twelve sons. Their descendants became the twelve tribes of Israel. Through the tribe of Judah came a young virgin named Mary. She gave birth to a tiny baby named Jesus, the Messiah, who brought salvation to every tribe, tongue, and people in the world.

"Through your offspring all nations on earth will be blessed," God told Abraham (Genesis 22:18).

And blessed indeed are we.

My fretful, tormented time of decision-making as a young adult ultimately led me to recognize how much I needed God's wisdom. I surrendered my life to His control and have never looked back.

Uncommon Power

God eagerly responds to the sincere, godly, faith-filled prayers of His children asking for direction.

Praise Prompt

Father, I praise you for honoring your Word and your principles. When we seek to follow and obey you, you show up in mighty ways. Thank you for Eliezer's example of devoted servanthood. Help me serve you, my Master, as faithfully as he served his. In the strong name of Jesus I ask, amen.

Live It Out

Are you struggling with a decision and unsure of which path to take? Why not follow Eliezer's example? As you obey what God has already told you, pray specifically, worship God, and tell others about your experience, the same God who answered Eliezer's cry for help will also answer yours.

44

When You're Afraid

Save me, I pray.

GENESIS 32:11

Jacob was scared. Really, really scared.

He was headed home, but that wasn't necessarily a good thing. Twenty years earlier he had fled from his father's house and his brother's murderous presence.

"As soon as Dad dies," Esau had vowed, "I will kill you." And he meant it.

Now, after decades of self-imposed exile, Jacob was coming home and bringing his family with him. Granted, he was a new man. Years of spiritual growth had transformed him from a conniving, self-centered mama's boy into a man of integrity and courage.

But Esau didn't know that. As far as he knew, Jacob was still the manipulative weasel who had stolen his blessing—and the one he had promised to kill.

No wonder Jacob found it hard to sleep the night before he encountered his brother. The faces of his young children hovered before his eyes every time he closed them. He saw his wives' faces too—the women he'd promised to love and protect. What if his risky actions endangered those he loved most?

But instead of figuring out a way to avoid an encounter with his brother, as the old Jacob would have done, he did what the new Jacob had learned to do—he prayed.

Let's look at Jacob's prayer, as recorded in Genesis 32. In it we can discover powerful principles to apply to any anxiety-producing situation.

Jacob first acknowledged God's faithfulness in the past. He began his prayer, "O God of my father Abraham, God of my father Isaac" (v. 9). By doing this, he reminded himself that God had been faithful to his family for three generations. He had kept the promises He had made to them. Jacob could trust Him.

Then Jacob realized God had brought him to this place. He recognized God as the one "who said to me, 'Go back to your country and your relatives, and I will make you prosper'" (v. 9). He reminded the Lord (my paraphrase), "I'm in this scary place, with my uncertain future, because I obeyed you."

The same is often true in our lives today. Obeying God doesn't guarantee we'll avoid frightening places. However, as Billy Graham often said, "The will of God will never take us where the grace of God cannot sustain us."[15]

But what if we find ourselves in a precarious place because we've disobeyed or ignored God's direction? Are we on our own? Thankfully, no. God also hears and answers the honest prayer of a repentant heart.

Jacob humbled himself. He understood that all he had and all he had become was because of God's mercy and grace. "I am unworthy of all the kindness and faithfulness you have shown your servant," he prayed. "I had only my staff when I crossed this Jordan, but now I have become two camps" (v. 10).

The same is true for us. Acknowledging that God is the source of our blessings protects us from an ungrateful, entitled mindset.

Next, Jacob asked boldly. "Save me, I pray, from the hand of my brother Esau" (v. 11). Despite his precarious position and Esau's superior strength, he boldly asked God to protect him and his family.

Like Jacob, we sometimes find ourselves in impossible situations with the odds stacked against us. We, too, can ask the God of miracles to do the unimaginable.

Jacob also acknowledged his fears. "I am afraid he will come and attack me, and also the mothers with their children" (v. 11). There is no need to hide our fears from God. He knows our hearts better than we do. Honest transparency unburdens our hearts and draws us closer to the Lord, whose shoulders are broad enough to bear our burdens.

Finally, Jacob trusted the promises God had given him. He concluded his prayer this way: "But you have said, 'I will surely make you prosper and will make your descendants like the sand of the sea'" (v. 12). By recounting to the Lord (not because God had forgotten, but because Jacob needed to remember) the specific promises God had given him, Jacob's faith grew stronger.

When we pray back to God appropriate promises that fit our situation, our faith grows stronger too. By claiming the promises in God's Word, we remember God is a covenant-making, promise-keeping God who encourages His children to call on Him.

If you're familiar with the story, you know God honored Jacob's prayer. He protected him from harm and restored his relationship with his brother. Most important, God preserved the family line that would one day lead to the Messiah, the Savior of Israel.

Uncommon Power

God's past faithfulness and future promises enable us to face each fear with courage.

Praise Prompt

Father, we praise you for your sovereign control over all of our circumstances, even our times of failure and sin. Thank you for using flawed men and women to teach us powerful life principles. I praise you for preserving Israel, your chosen people, and adopting us into your spiritual family. When I am afraid, help me pray as Jacob prayed and see your mighty hand at work on my behalf.

Live It Out

Whatever you're facing today, remember God's faithfulness. Acknowledge He has brought you to this place. Approach Him humbly, ask boldly, speak honestly, and trust the promises He has given you. By praying as Jacob did, you can access God's power and watch Him answer in ways that bring Him glory.

45

Praying for Unbelievers

**The Lord opened her heart to
respond to Paul's message.**

ACTS 16:14

Think of someone you care about who doesn't know Christ as their Savior.

If you're like me, every time you think of this person, your heart aches. You know if they don't accept Christ, they'll die and spend eternity in hell. I'm so afraid someone I love might spend eternity separated from God (and from me). May it never be.

But the reality is that one day we'll all stand before the judgment seat of Christ and give an account. The entrance exam to heaven has one question:

In whom are you trusting?

There's only one right answer: "I'm trusting in Jesus Christ as my Savior."

For years I couldn't give this answer. The best I could do was hope my good works outweighed my bad works on judgment day (an impossibility). Some of my acquaintances, friends, and loved ones can't give this answer because they haven't yet come to faith in Jesus Christ. They're still trusting in their works to get them into heaven. They don't understand the truth of Ephesians 2:8–9: "For it is by grace you have been saved, through faith—and this is not from yourselves, it is the gift of God—not by works, so that no one can boast."

Sadly, some aren't interested in heaven at all. Having a relationship with God is the furthest thing from their minds. Like King Solomon, they spend their lives seeking pleasure and everything else this world has to offer. They have no idea that a far greater joy is possible through faith in Christ.

Because I love these precious people, I share my faith with them, serve them, and do my best to demonstrate God's love. But the most important thing I can do is pray for them.

Pastor and theologian J. Sidlow Baxter once said, "Men may spurn our appeals, reject our message, oppose our arguments, despise our persons; but they are helpless against our prayers."[16]

One of the most powerful ways we can pray for our lost loved ones is to ask God to open their hearts to believe. The Bible tells us no one comes to Jesus unless the Father draws him (John 6:65), so it makes sense to ask God to draw our loved ones to himself and open their hearts to place their faith in Christ.

The book of Acts tells of a woman named Lydia. She was a religious woman who worshiped God, but she hadn't yet trusted Jesus as her Savior. When Paul shared the gospel with her, something miraculous happened. Acts 16:14 describes it this way:

"The Lord opened her heart to respond to Paul's message."

Apart from God opening a person's heart to believe, the message of the gospel falls on deaf ears. The spiritually dead can't receive the life-giving truths of Scripture unless God opens their hearts. This is what we should pray for.

The takeaway from Acts 16 is simple: Pray for the people you love who don't know Christ as their Savior. When you pray, ask God to unlock their hearts to the life-giving message of the gospel.

Pray and don't stop.

"For it is with your heart that you believe and are justified, and it is with your mouth that you profess your faith and are saved" (Romans 10:10).

Uncommon Power

God is the one who opens a person's heart to receive the message of the gospel, and He hears your prayers for your loved one. Don't give up.

Praise Prompt

I praise you, Father, for your amazing grace. Through no merit of our own, you draw us to yourself, open our hearts to believe, and invite us into a relationship with you. Thank you for also loving those I love, for dying on the cross for them, for pursuing them and offering them the opportunity to have a relationship with you. I'm so grateful that I can trust you with those I hold dear.

Live It Out

When you feel tempted to worry or fret about your unsaved loved ones, pray instead. Ask God to remove the spiritual blinders from their eyes so they can see their need for a relationship with Him.

Pray for a spiritual restlessness to come upon them that won't allow them to be satisfied until their souls find rest in Him. Invite God to work in their lives, drawing them to himself and opening their hearts to believe.

46

If Your Loved Ones Still Aren't Saved

The Lord is not slow in keeping his promise,
as some understand slowness. Instead he
is patient with you, not wanting anyone to
perish, but everyone to come to repentance.

2 PETER 3:9

Have you been praying for a friend or loved one for years—or maybe decades? Despite your fervent prayers, do they seem no closer to Jesus than the day you uttered your first petition?

They might even seem more lost than ever, reaping the consequences of their poor choices and struggling against the undertow of their sin. Or worse—they're enjoying the fruit of prosperity, oblivious to their need for a Savior.

Do you ever grow disheartened? Do you wonder if your prayers are accomplishing anything? God's going to save who He's going to save, you think, so why bother praying, crying, and hoping?

God *is* going to save who He's going to save, and this truth gives me great hope. And He will use my prayers to help bring about that transformation.

Our prayers aren't useless; otherwise God wouldn't tell us to pray. But sometimes we grow weary. If you're one of the weary ones, committed to praying but struggling against doubt and discouragement, here are four things to remember:

1. You can pray in confidence and trust God's heart. While not everyone will come to faith in Christ, God's invitation is open to everyone. He'll do everything possible to draw those He's called to himself (2 Peter 3:9). He won't turn away anyone who wants to place their faith in Christ.

2. No heart is too hard for God. The apostle Paul testified, "Here is a trustworthy saying that deserves full acceptance: Christ Jesus came into the world to save sinners—of whom I am the worst" (1 Timothy 1:15). Paul blasphemed the name of Christ and hunted down and murdered untold number of Christians. He did everything within his power to wipe Christianity from the face of the earth. By his own testimony, he was the baddest of the bad. Yet God saved him. No matter what our loved ones have done or how hard they seem, God can still remove their stony hearts and give them hearts of flesh (Ezekiel 11:19).

3. Your prayers reach beyond your lifetime. Even if your prayers go unanswered in this lifetime, they can still extend into the future. After your death, your prayers will continue to work on your loved one's behalf. Heroes of the faith like Moses, Solomon, and Daniel prayed for future generations and asked God to draw them to himself.

Based on Deuteronomy 7:9, my husband and I often ask God to extend His saving grace to a thousand generations of our family: "Know therefore that the LORD your God is God; he is the faithful God, keeping his covenant of love to a thousand generations of those who love him and keep his commandments." We pray for our grandchildren's salvation, for their future spouses' salvation, and the salvation of the generations yet to come, through time, until Jesus comes back.

4. Even if you don't live near your loved one, God's people are everywhere. We see a beautiful example of this at Paul's conversion. God spoke to Paul apart from the influence of a sermon, preacher, or Christian witness. After Paul received faith, God sent Ananias, a believer, to explain the next steps and baptize him.

Sometimes, if we're the only Christian in our family or circle of influence, we think our loved ones' salvation depends on us. If we don't witness to them, no one else will. While we should use every opportunity God gives us to share our faith, we might live far away or they might resist our efforts. Maybe the opportunities for spiritual conversations are rare or limited.

While God often uses a believing family member or friend to lead someone to Christ, He isn't limited by time, distance, or manpower. God has the world's resources at His disposal and can use anything and anyone. When you pray for your lost loved ones, ask God to bring bold, winsome, dynamic believers into their lives.

God saves those He's going to save, and, by God's mercy and grace, we get to be a part of His work. He invites us, through the soul sweat of prayer, to come alongside Him as He draws our loved ones to himself.

Pray on, dear heart. "Let us not become weary in doing good, for at the proper time we will reap a harvest if we do not give up" (Galatians 6:9).

Uncommon Power

We needn't despair when our lost loved ones are long in coming to Christ. God hears our prayers and will answer them in His wisdom and timing.

Praise Prompt

God, I praise you that you came into the world to save sinners. Thank you for loving those dearest to me even more than I do. Help me rest in your unfailing love—for me and for them.

Live It Out

Do you find yourself giving up praying for certain loved ones? Or maybe you continue to pray, but your prayers lack hope? Ask God to give you a renewed passion to pray for these loved ones and new insights into their needs. Ask Him to soften your loved one's heart and draw them to himself.

47

Praying Whenever God Prompts

**I cried to the LORD with my voice,
and He heard me from His holy hill.**

PSALM 3:4 (NKJV)

When I was a little girl, my grandmother taught me to pray whenever I heard a siren. "Fire trucks, police cars, and ambulances mean someone needs help," she'd say, "so always say a prayer." I took her words to heart and have prayed for people who need rescuing all my life. I taught my daughters to do the same. Now I'm teaching my grandchildren.

One evening four-year-old Caroline, two-year-old Andrew, and I were sitting on the front porch. A storm was brewing, and we could hear thunder to our west.

Aware that children are often frightened by thunder and lightning, I used the coming storm as a teaching opportunity.

"We don't have to be afraid of thunder," I said. "It's just warm and cold air bumping together and making noise. But we do have to respect lightning. You never want to be out in the open during a storm."

As if on cue, a bright light crackled in the distance. More thunder rumbled. Then, over the noise, we heard a different sound—high pitched and urgent. Caroline recognized it first.

"That's a ambulance, Gigi."

Another insistent wail joined the first. Then another. And another.

"And those are fire trucks," I said. "We'd better pray for the people who need them."

We closed our eyes and prayed.

"Dear Jesus, please be with the people who need the fire trucks and the ambulance. We don't know who they are, but you do. Help them be okay. And keep the firemen safe too."

"And if the people don't know Jesus . . ." Caroline added, opening one eye, and looking at me to finish the familiar prayer.

". . . send someone to tell them about you. In Jesus's name we ask, amen."

We went inside, ate dinner, and settled down to play Candy Land when my daughter glanced at her phone. "Oh no!" she said. "There's a house on fire in our neighborhood." Clicking and swiping for a closer look at the news photo, she quickly determined it wasn't their house, and we breathed a sigh of relief.

But then our thoughts went to the family whose home *was* on fire.

"Caroline!" I said. "Remember the sirens we heard? Those fire trucks must have been on their way to your neighborhood. Maybe the house was struck by lightning. I'm so glad we prayed for them."

Later we learned that the family, including the cat, escaped with no injuries.

Many times when God prompts me to pray, I never learn what the outcome is. I pray blindly, in faith. I seldom know the situation, the need, or the person for whom I'm praying. I just pray, trusting that God, who knows all the details, will apply my prayers as needed.

Last week, however, was a different story. For whatever reason, God cracked the curtain on our prayers and revealed exactly who we were praying for.

Maybe He allowed it to grow my or my grandchildren's faith.

Regardless, I'm even more committed to praying for fire trucks, ambulances, and police cars. For school buses, city buses, and the people who drive down my street. For walkers, joggers, and the children who attend the nearby school.

Who knows how God wants to use my prayers? Who knows how He wants to use yours? I'm thankful God invites us to pray for our friends, family, and the people we interact with every day. I'm also grateful for the chance to pray for people we don't know. When we pray for strangers, we model God's love for mankind and invite Him to work in their lives.

Uncommon Power

While we may not always know the people we pray for, God knows them and cares about them enough to prompt us to pray for their needs.

Praise Prompt

Father, thank you for the times you allow me to see evidence that my prayers are making a difference. This encourages me to persevere and keep praying, even when I don't see the results. I praise you for being intimately aware of all those you have created and for moving in the hearts of believers to intercede for them in their time of need. Your wisdom is unfathomable, and your power immense.

Live It Out

Have you ever prayed for someone you didn't know? A stranger you passed on the road or a person you've never met? Today, view every encounter with someone, no matter how brief, as an invitation to pray for them. Then trust the Holy Spirit to apply your prayers to their area of greatest need.

48

Praying for the Bride of Christ

Pray in the Spirit on all occasions with
all kinds of prayers and requests.
With this in mind, be alert and always keep
on praying for all the Lord's people.

EPHESIANS 6:18

When my brother-in-law, Luther, came to faith in Christ soon after he was diagnosed with lung cancer, our church welcomed him as the long-lost family member he was. My husband, David, had been praying for his big brother for twenty-six years. The church had been praying with him.

When Luther surrendered his life to Jesus, those who had prayed with us for so long rejoiced. Surrounded by his new church family, Luther was baptized in an outdoor ceremony. As the pastor lowered him beneath the water and raised him up again, he declared, "Buried with Christ in baptism. Raised to walk in newness of life."

Luther, normally a stoic, couldn't contain the joy that welled up in his heart. He raised his arms toward heaven and shouted, "Hallelujah!"

"Hallelujah!" the church responded. "Praise God!"

Our church loved, discipled, and supported him. One member paid to build a wheelchair ramp when he grew too weak to walk. Others gave him rides to Bible study, invited him to dinner, and included him in men-only weekends. When he was admitted to the hospital under hospice care, the men from his study group gathered around his bed to study the Bible one last time with him.

When Luther went home to be with the Lord, the church was there. One family donated his burial vault. Another organized a meal after the service. The pastor who had guided Luther's spiritual growth shared a heartfelt, moving eulogy. Members we didn't even know waited in a long line to express their condolences and share hugs.

Eight months later, when David's sister, Kay, died of a brain aneurysm, the church was there. We were four thousand miles away leading a mission team in Mexico and couldn't come back for the funeral. Church friends did what we couldn't do—helped with arrangements, ministered to our devastated family, and stood in our place at Kay's funeral.

Three weeks later, the church did it all again when my sister, Cindy, died.

Some say the church is for weddings and funerals, and it is. But the church is so much more. Locally and worldwide, the church is the restraining force of evil in this world. It's the vehicle God has ordained to take the gospel to the lost and bring help to the redeemed. It's the hands and feet of Jesus.

The church is a force for societal transformation, but it's also our only hope for spiritual transformation. Social programs address the symptoms of a sin-sick world, but the gospel, shared through the church, changes hearts.

Today's church is flawed, frail, and floundering, but it is still the bride of Christ, beloved of God and holy. Jesus loved the church so much He died for it (Ephesians 5:25).

This is why we must pray for the church. Although God could have called people to salvation all by himself, He chose the church, the worldwide family of believers, to carry His gospel to the uttermost parts of the earth.

As you pray for your church and the church around the world, consider these ten requests.

Pray the church will be faithful and obedient to:

1. Proclaim the truth of God's Word in love and without compromise (2 Timothy 4:2).

2. Share the gospel with boldness and power (Acts 4:12).

3. Remain deeply committed to prayer (Colossians 4:2).

4. Call godly men and women to serve the body and lead by example (Ephesians 4:11–12).

5. Remain pure and separated from the world and its evil influences (James 1:27).

6. Grow in wisdom, maturity, and influence (Colossians 1:28–29).

7. Remain faithful to Jesus, its first love (Revelation 2:4–5).

8. Rely on God and trust His timing and direction as He builds the church (Matthew 16:18).

9. Recognize and reject Satan's schemes (2 Corinthians 11:3).

10. Shine the light of Christ into our dark world (Matthew 5:14–16).

As we enjoy the blessings that come from being a member of God's family, let's also remember the responsibilities. We are privileged to pray and participate.

Uncommon Power

Although the church is flawed and frail, it remains the vehicle God has chosen to bring the gospel to the world. We, as its members, must faithfully pray for its health and vitality.

Praise Prompt

Lord, you gave your church a weighty task—to preach the gospel to all people—and our mission isn't complete. Open doors, we pray, for your Word to go forth. Help us boldly proclaim the mystery of the gospel. Add to our numbers daily, Lord, those who will be saved. Empower us to serve each other as if we were serving you. Help us love in your name and stand for what is right, even when it costs us. Make us bold and courageous witnesses—for your glory.

Live It Out

If you haven't regularly prayed for the church, begin today. Use the ten items above as a starting point. Read the accompanying verses and pray them back to God. Pray for your church leaders, then drop them a note or send them a text to let them know you're praying for them.

49

How Long, O Lord?

When he opened the fifth seal, I saw
under the altar the souls of those who
had been slain because of the word
of God and the testimony they had
maintained. They called out in a loud
voice, "How long, Sovereign Lord, holy
and true, until you judge the inhabitants
of the earth and avenge our blood?"

REVELATION 6:9–10

One hundred thousand animal lovers signed a petition spearheaded by the Chicago French Bulldog Rescue to prevent fifteen Frenchie puppies from being deported to Jordan. The puppies, snuck into the country by a Russian breeder, were found in a Chicago warehouse starving, dehydrated, and diseased. One puppy died in the deplorable conditions when the CDC rejected the dogs' forged paperwork, leaving them to languish in the hot warehouse with no food or water for three days.

When I heard of the puppies' plight and the government's attempt to send them back to the breeder who committed the travesty, anger rose within me. When my daughter, a French bulldog owner herself, showed me pictures of their tiny snub-nosed faces wearing miniature medical cones, my heart broke. Righteous indignation and a desire to defend and protect the helpless creatures moved me to act and pray on behalf of the #Jordan15.

Anyone with a heart would feel the same way I did. Yet an even greater travesty exists in the world today. More despicable than animal neglect are the crimes committed against millions of Christians around the world. At the time of this writing, Open Doors reports 340 million Christians worldwide suffer severe persecution simply for believing in Jesus.[17] That's one in eight believers.

Fifteen neglected puppies made my heart crack open, but 340 *million* brothers and sisters in Christ beaten, tortured, and killed? When I picture two tiny puppies stuffed into a crate and wallowing in their own filth, my stomach churns. Yet believers in hostile countries like China and Iran often find themselves imprisoned in far worse conditions.

When I imagine pointy-eared puppies whimpering because their bellies are empty and their throats parched, I want authorities to punish the guilty. Around the globe, however, persecuted believers lose their jobs and the ability to feed their families every day while their tormentors go unpunished.

Until my daughter shared the Frenchies' plight, I didn't know to act or pray. Hearing their story and seeing their faces changed everything. I felt this way when I learned about the Voice of the Martyrs ministry.[18] When I visited their website, I saw the faces of persecuted believers and read their prayer requests.

Instead of asking for deliverance, these brave men and women ask for courage to stay strong when they are abused and for faith to fearlessly proclaim the gospel. Instead of asking for punishment for their tormentors, they pray for God to give them the ability to love them in Jesus's name and to shine the light of Christ in the dark places where they live.

As I read their stories and learned their names, I discovered how to act and pray on their behalf. I grieved for their suffering. I wept over their trials. I rejoiced in their victories. When I heard that a pastor had been released from prison and aid had come to refugees fleeing an evil regime, I felt as though I, too, had been rescued. In a way, I had. First Corinthians 12:12, 26 reminds us, "Just as a body, though one, has many parts, but all its many parts form one body, so it is with Christ. . . . If one part suffers, every part suffers with it; if one part is honored, every part rejoices with it."

As the political and social climate in our country grows colder and more antagonistic toward Christians, we may one day join the family of persecuted believers. I pray we don't, but if God gives us the privilege of suffering for His name, we must be ready. As we pray for courage, faith, protection, and perseverance for the persecuted church, we must pray this for ourselves as well.

"Remember those in prison," Paul reminded us from his own jail cell, "as if you were together with them in prison, and those who are mistreated as if you yourselves were suffering" (Hebrews 13:3).

Because dedicated animal lovers championed the fifteen French bulldog puppies' cause and raised awareness of their plight, the US government chose not to deport them. Instead, they released them for adoption into loving homes. Similarly, when we respond to God's prompting to pray for the 340 million persecuted believers around the world, God meets their needs in ways we can only imagine. Some are released. Others are empowered to hold fast to their faith and share Jesus with those around them.

Uncommon Power

God uses our prayers to strengthen and deliver our persecuted brothers and sisters around the world.

Praise Prompt

Father, when I think about some of the earliest persecuted believers, I remember how Paul and Silas rejoiced because they were counted worthy to suffer in your name. O Lord, instill this mindset into the hearts and minds of our brothers and sisters throughout the world. We praise you for granting them courage, faith, and stamina to stay strong in the face of opposition. Thank you for standing with them as they stand for Christ. May you be glorified in and through them, and may many come to believe in you because of their witness. In the mighty name of Jesus I pray, amen.

Live It Out

How often do you pray for the persecuted church? If you haven't prayed regularly, add them to your prayer schedule. Visit the Voice of the Martyrs (www.persecution.com) for specific names and prayer requests.

50

His Kingdom Come

**Your kingdom come, your will be done,
on earth as it is in heaven.**

MATTHEW 6:10

"Once upon a time, in a land far away, lived a mighty king."

I don't know how many times I've read these words to my children, and now, to my grandchildren. The concept of a royal leader, sovereign over the affairs of a kingdom, strong and good, fascinates them.

It fascinates me too.

Unlike the heroes of their fairy tales, who reign from the pages of storybooks and come to life only on movie screens, my Sovereign rules over a literal kingdom—one that was, and is, and is to come.

The NIV translation mentions *kingdom* 114 times in the Gospels. The book of Matthew alone contains fifty-two references to this mysterious kingdom. Perhaps the most famous of these is stitched into the middle of the Lord's Prayer. As Jesus taught His disciples to pray, He urged them to ask for His kingdom to come.

Why?

Old Testament Scriptures acknowledge that God's kingdom—His rule and reign—existed long before the incarnate Christ walked the earth. "The LORD has established his throne in heaven," King David wrote, "and his kingdom rules over all" (Psalm 103:19). God has always governed and controlled the vast expanse of His created world.

When the Pharisees asked Christ when the kingdom of God would come, He answered, "Behold, the kingdom of God is in the midst of you" (Luke 17:21 ESV).

If God's kingdom has always been, and, when Christ walked the earth, existed in the midst of them, why did Jesus call men to pray, "your kingdom come"?

Herein lies the mystery of God's reign—His kingdom is past, present, and future. Already, but not yet.

When God formed the world, He placed Adam and Eve in a perfect environment. In history past, God's kingdom *was.*

When sin marred His creation and plunged it into death and decay, His kingdom took on a new dimension. God set into motion His plan to conquer sin, Satan, and death through Christ's sacrifice on the cross. When we surrender our lives to Jesus and call upon Him for salvation, His kingdom comes in our hearts. We become citizens of an otherworldly realm. In history present, God's kingdom *is.*

Once we know Christ as Savior, we join the host of believers down through the ages who await His future and final kingdom—the kingdom that is *to come.*

God has always intended to save a people for himself and renew and restore the world sin had corrupted. We catch a glimpse of what we look forward to in Revelation 21:1–3.

> Then I saw "a new heaven and a new earth," for the first heaven and the first earth had passed away . . . I saw the Holy City, the new Jerusalem, coming down out of heaven from God, prepared as a bride beautifully dressed for her husband. And I heard a loud voice from the throne saying, "Look! God's dwelling place is now among the people, and he will dwell with them. They will be his people."

When we pray, we ask God to draw people to himself and save them. This establishes His kingdom in the hearts of men and women. When all whom God has ordained for salvation come to faith, God's final, perfect, and everlasting kingdom will begin. What a day that will be!

"'God himself will be with them and be their God. "He will wipe every tear from their eyes. There will be no more death" or mourning or crying or pain, for the old order of things has passed away.' He who was seated on the throne said, 'I am making everything new!'" (vv. 3–5).

This is why God calls us to pray, "Your kingdom come, your will be done, on earth as it is in heaven."

Uncommon Power

As we pray for God's kingdom to come, we help usher in our own glorious future.

Praise Prompt

Father, my heart soars as I think about how your kingdom was, and is, and is to come. Thank you for including me in your family, allowing me to be a part of your work here on earth, and, one day, bringing me with you to live in your forever kingdom. I long for that day. May your kingdom come!

Live It Out

Have you ever pondered the words, "your kingdom come"? Do you pray for God to bring to fruition His plan to redeem and restore the world? If so, keep praying. If not, begin today.

Part 6

Favorite Prayers from the Bible

51

Moses's Prayer for More of God

Show me your glory.

EXODUS 33:18

Completing a high-ropes course had always been on my bucket list but not on my friend Maryann's. When we spotted the course dangling above the deck of the cruise ship like a spider web, several of us decided to try it.

Our excited chatter sucked Maryann in. She saw the harness, the anchor cable, and the spotters and concluded it must be safe. Her enthusiasm waned, however, the closer we got to the entrance.

Most high-ropes courses are stationary, suspended twenty to thirty feet above the ground. This one hung above the bow of the moving ship. To add to the challenge, a gusty wind blew, tossing the ropes and buffeting the climbers.

"I'm not so sure about this," Maryann said as an attendant strapped her into a harness. "It's so high. And so wobbly. And *so scary!*"

"I'll go ahead of you," I promised. "I'll show you where to put your feet and where to grab hold."

"And I'll be right behind you," another friend chimed in. "I'll cheer you on."

Glancing at the long line queueing up behind her, she took a deep breath.

"Okay, but don't leave me." With friends before and behind her, she stepped out.

Like Maryann, Moses faced an overwhelming situation. God called him to lead more than a million reluctant, often rebellious Israelites through the desert to the promised land. This was a task that would make even the bravest doubt.

"If your Presence does not go with us," Moses told God, "do not send us up from here" (Exodus 33:15).

Despite God's reassurance that He would go before them, Moses remained afraid. He'd seen God's judgment fall on the idolatrous Israelites. He knew they were stubborn and rebellious. He feared God might sweep the desert with them the next time they angered Him.

In a display of uncharacteristic boldness, Moses asked for something no one had ever asked for before.

"Show me your glory" (v. 18).

Moses had heard God's promises, but he needed to see God's nature. Was He trustworthy? Would He extend His grace? Would He carry them through the wilderness? Or would He abandon them the next time the Israelites sinned—because Moses knew they would.

In a characteristic expression of grace, God agreed.

"I will cause all my goodness to pass in front of you, and I will proclaim my name, the LORD, in your presence" (v. 19).

Then, to prove He was trustworthy, God took Moses high up on the mountain, hid him in a cleft of the rock, and allowed him to witness His glory.

"And he passed in front of Moses, proclaiming, 'The Lord, the Lord, the compassionate and gracious God, slow to anger, abounding in love and faithfulness, maintaining love to thousands, and forgiving wickedness, rebellion and sin. Yet he does not leave the guilty unpunished'" (34:6–7).

God described himself to Moses as merciful, gracious, longsuffering, good, true, forgiving, and just. God's name, which encompasses the essence of His character, reassured Moses that He would walk with the Israelites all the way through the wilderness wanderings and into the promised land.

Like Moses and Maryann, we often face frightening situations that seem insurmountable. We know, without a trustworthy guide, we have no hope. Suspended between the sea and the sky, Maryann trusted her friends—our good name and the promises we made to her. Suspended between Egypt and the promised land, Moses trusted in God's glory, revealed through His good name.

As He did for Moses, God invites us to pray, "Show me your glory." Every time we do, He reveals a bit of himself to us. Sometimes He sends the insight we need to take a wobbly faith step. Or He provides for our needs in unexpected ways. Sometimes He bridges emotional gulfs to restore severed relationships. Most precious of all, He turns the eyes of our souls toward himself so we can see Him, high and lifted up, ruling supreme over the affairs of our lives.

Moses wasn't the only one who saw glimpses of God's glory. First-century Israel saw it, too, in the face of Jesus. Listen to the apostle John's description: "The Word became flesh and made his dwelling among us. We have seen his glory, the glory of the one and only Son, who came from the Father, full of grace and truth" (John 1:14).

One day we won't have to depend on Bible stories or someone else's description of God's glory. We'll see Him with our own eyes. "We know that when Christ appears," John said, "we shall be like him, for *we shall see him as he is*" (1 John 3:2).

Imagine that.

Until then, we'll pray Moses's prayer, take courage from the glimpses we see, and yearn for the day when we see Him in all His transcendent glory.

Uncommon Power

We see glimpses of God's glory here on earth, but one day we will see Him face to face. This allows us to pray as Moses did, asking God to reveal himself to us.

Praise Prompt

Father, your Word tells us, "You cannot see my face, for no one may see me and live," yet you reveal yourself to us every day through your Word, your character, and your promises. Help us come boldly before your throne to ask for more of You. May we never be satisfied with just one glimpse. Instead, help us seek your face every day through prayer and your Word.

Live It Out

Have you ever asked God to show you His glory? Do you yearn for a deeper understanding of Him? Begin today to pray, as Moses did, for God to reveal himself to you. Then watch to see how He speaks to you through His Word, godly friends, and the Holy Spirit. Record these glimpses in your Bible or journal.

52

Moses's Prayer of Discouragement

I cannot carry all these people by myself;
the burden is too heavy for me.

NUMBERS 11:14

I've always admired Moses. One of the first superheroes of the Bible, Moses was strong, brave, and smart. With the help of his sidekick brother, Aaron, God called him to challenge the greatest power on earth, emancipate more than a million people, draft and implement a national government, and lead Israel for forty years through the wilderness into the promised land.

And did I mention that he was humble? The humblest man on earth, according to Numbers 12:3. What's not to like about Moses? Aside from a few temper tantrums, he was, as Mary Poppins would say, "Practically perfect in every way."

While I've admired him from afar, I've never identified with him. I have nothing in common with practically perfect people. For years he sat, aloof and shining, on my Heroes of the Faith shelf.

Until Numbers 11.

The events of Numbers 11 removed Moses from the untouchable shelf and put him in the corner of my heart reserved for my dearest friends.

Picture the scene. The Israelites had tromped around the desert for several years. While their shoes and clothing hadn't worn out, their spirits had grown weary. They whined and complained about everything and everyone.

Numbers 11 opens with a complaint. The carnivores among them had grown tired of the manna God had so faithfully provided. "If only we had meat to eat!" they wailed. "We remember the fish we ate in Egypt at no cost—also the cucumbers, melons, leeks, onions and garlic. But now we have lost our appetite; we never see anything but this manna!" (vv. 4–6)

Maybe Moses hadn't had his quiet time that morning, or perhaps he'd missed his second cup of coffee. Regardless, he lost it.

"Why have you brought this trouble on your servant?" he complained to God. "What have I done to displease you that you put the burden of all these people on me? Did I conceive all these people? Did I give them birth? Why do you tell me to carry them in my arms, as a nurse carries an infant, to the land you promised on oath to their ancestors? Where can I get meat for all these people? They keep wailing to me, 'Give us meat to eat!'" (vv. 11–13)

Listen to Moses's desperation: "I cannot carry all these people by myself," he cried. "The burden is too heavy for me. If this is how you are going to treat me, please go ahead and kill me—if I have found favor in your eyes—and do not let me face my own ruin" (vv. 14–15).

Can you identify with Moses? Overwhelmed. Exhausted. Miserable. *If this is what life is going to look like for the foreseeable future, just kill me now.*

I often felt like an utter failure during my child-rearing years. My children's never-ending needs, combined with my lack of patience, wisdom, and godliness drowned me in discouragement. A difficult season of marriage, a period of financial difficulty, or the strain of balancing the demands of our lives often prompts us to say to the Lord, "The burden is too heavy for me!"

Knowing mighty Moses felt this way helps me identify with him. It also gives me hope. If someone so emotionally strong and godly could come unraveled, perhaps my frailty isn't so shameful after all.

I love how God responded to Moses's prayer. He didn't scold him for feeling overwhelmed. He didn't send him back up on the mountain to memorize more Scripture. And contrary to what Moses requested, He didn't kill him.

Instead, He sent help—seventy wise men filled with the Spirit to ease his burden and help him lead.

Sometimes I forget God is my greatest ally. That I can come to Him when I feel overwhelmed and ask for help. That I don't have to carry the burdens of my life alone. When I pray to him, He hears and answers, reminding me that in my weakness, He is strong (2 Corinthians 12:9).

Uncommon Power

When I feel overwhelmed, I can call out to God and ask Him to supply everything I need to do what He's called me to do.

Praise Prompt

Father, thank you that I don't have to operate in my own strength. I'm grateful I can cry out to you when I feel undone. I can ask for help and know you hear me. Thank you for sending others into my life to lift my tired arms and refresh my weary soul. When I feel like giving up, thank you for giving me the strength to carry on in faith, confident that you who have begun a good work in me will be faithful to complete it (Philippians 1:6).

Live It Out

If you're feeling like Moses today, don't despair. Cry out to God in faith. Trust Him to provide what you need just when you need it.

53

David's Prayer
of Gratitude

**Who am I, Sovereign Lord, and what is my
family, that you have brought me this far?**

2 SAMUEL 7:18

When my self-righteous nature surfaces, I find myself looking down my nose at Israel's King David. How can Scripture refer to him as "a man after [God's] own heart" (Acts 13:22)?

He began well as the nation's champion, slaying the blasphemous Goliath and courageously commanding Israel's army. He refused to kill King Saul, trusting God to appoint him king instead of seizing the position. But then he let his guard down. He grew lazy and complacent. One sin led to another until he added *adulterer* and *murderer* to his official résumé.

Yet despite his moral failings, God still called David His friend.

The psalms David wrote bear witness to his courage, devotion, tenderheartedness, and reverence. I'm sure God smiled on all these attributes, but David's most notable characteristic was his humble gratitude. We see this quality manifest itself in a story recorded in the book of 2 Samuel.

In his later years, David wanted to build a temple for God.

"Here I am," he said to Nathan the prophet, "living in a house of cedar, while the ark of God remains in a tent" (7:2). God had given David victory over his enemies and allowed him to amass great quantities of gold, silver, and precious articles. Some he used to build his own palace, but the majority he set aside to build a house of worship, a temple for his God.

David described his plans to Nathan, who pronounced his blessing on the project.

But God said no.

"You are not to build a house for my Name, because you are a warrior and have shed blood" (1 Chronicles 28:3).

Yet, with tender mercies, God softened His no with a promise: "When your days are over and you rest with your ancestors, I will raise up your offspring to succeed you, your own flesh and blood, and I will establish his kingdom. He is the one who will build a house for my Name, and I will establish the throne of his kingdom forever" (2 Samuel 7:12–13).

David's response was equally tender. He walked into the tabernacle and sat before the Lord. I picture David taking the jeweled crown from his head and setting it aside, shrugging off the gold-edged robe, and prostrating himself before the altar.

With his face in his hands and tears of gratefulness flowing, he marveled aloud at God's goodness to him.

"Who am I, Sovereign Lord, and what is my family, that you have brought me this far? . . . How great you are, Sovereign Lord! There is no one like you, and there is no God but you" (vv. 18, 22).

When God rejected David's plan to build the temple, David could have reacted in anger or pride. Instead, he directed his grateful heart toward God, and his lips overflowed in praise.

When we experience life's disappointments, we, too, can choose gratitude. As Elisabeth Elliot, wife of martyred missionary Jim Elliot, said, "It's always possible to be thankful for what is given rather than to complain about what is not given. One or the other becomes a habit of life."[19]

David's response reveals he had schooled his heart in the discipline of gratitude. "The mouth speaks what the heart is full of," Luke 6:45 tells us.

Because gratitude doesn't come naturally, we have to learn it and practice it. In Psalm 103:2–5, we hear David talking to himself, focusing on God's goodness, and reminding himself to choose gratitude over grumbling: "Bless the LORD, O my soul, and forget not all His benefits: who forgives all your iniquities, who heals all your diseases, who redeems your life from destruction, who crowns you with lovingkindness and tender mercies, who satisfies your mouth with good things, so that your youth is renewed like the eagle's" (NKJV).

This is how David trained his heart and mind. Instead of concentrating on the negative aspects of his circumstances, David extolled the goodness of God *within* his circumstances.

We, too, can learn the art of humble gratitude. With practice and self-discipline, we can face disappointments with grace and reverence. We, too, can become a man or woman after God's own heart.

Uncommon Power

Even when life disappoints us, when we school our hearts in the benefits of God, we can respond with humble gratitude.

Praise Prompt

O Father, who are we that we should be called sons and daughters of God? We don't deserve your blessings. Anything good in us comes directly from you, for you have redeemed us, transformed us, and called us into your service. Banish all pride from our hearts and enable us to live lives of humble gratitude. In the mighty name of Jesus I ask, amen.

Live It Out

If you're struggling with disappointment, take time to ponder the goodness of God. In a journal or aloud in prayer, follow David's example. Challenge yourself to list some of God's characteristics that seem especially meaningful to you right now. You might mention His willingness to forgive, His ability to heal, or His loving-kindness and tender mercies. As you turn your eyes from yourself to God, allow the discipline of gratitude to soften the edges of your disappointment.

54

Solomon's Prayer for Wisdom

Give your servant a discerning heart to govern your people and to distinguish between right and wrong.

1 KINGS 3:9

Solomon and I have at least one thing in common—a healthy understanding of our own ignorance.

As an eighteen-year-old high school senior, I felt overwhelmed by the decisions that faced me. Where should I go to college? What should I study? Who should I date (and eventually marry)? I knew my choices would chart the course of my life, and I was terrified to make the wrong ones.

Many nights I couldn't sleep. I turned over one scenario after another in my mind. Early one morning, after a turbulent night, I arose from bed, looked in the mirror, and burst into tears.

"It's not fair," I wailed to my mom. "I'm only eighteen years old! I'm not smart enough to make these important decisions."

The book of 1 Kings describes another anxious young adult. King Solomon had just been appointed king over Israel. With the crown of responsibility resting heavily on his head, he felt the weight of every decision.

No doubt his father's words rang in his ears, "My son Solomon, the one whom God has chosen, is young and inexperienced. The task is great" (1 Chronicles 29:1). He also may have experienced a few sleepless nights, tossing and turning on his bed.

One night God appeared to him in a dream.

"Ask for whatever you want me to give you," God said (1 Kings 3:5).

Solomon was quick to reply. "Now, LORD my God, you have made your servant king in place of my father David. But I am only a little child and do not know how to carry out my duties. Your servant is here among the people you have chosen, a great people, too numerous to count or number. So give your servant a discerning heart to govern your people and to distinguish between right and wrong. For who is able to govern this great people of yours?" (vv. 7–9).

Solomon's request pleased the Lord. Not only did He grant Solomon a wise and understanding heart, He blessed him with riches and honor.

The apostle James encouraged New Testament believers to follow Solomon's example. "If any of you lacks wisdom," he wrote, "you should ask God, who gives generously to all and without finding fault, and it will be given to you" (James 1:5).

Like a wise father who desires to steer his children away from harm and toward the good path, God invites us to seek His wisdom for every decision we face.

As a young adult, I knew I needed someone wiser than myself to help me make crucial life choices. I sought the counsel of my pastor, who helped me realize I'd never fully surrendered my life to God's control. Once I did, I learned to seek God's wisdom instead of trusting my feelings or following my friends.

When I asked God for wisdom, He supplied the insight, guidance, and information I needed to move forward. Sometimes I'd read a relevant passage of Scripture I could apply to my situation. Other times a godly mentor or friend shared wise counsel. Sometimes snarly situations sorted themselves out. As I prayed, He provided insight to know what to do.

Our world swirls with confusing situations, conflicting opinions, and murky thinking. Our only hope for making God-honoring choices is to seek His wisdom every day. As He did with Solomon, God invites us to pray, "Give [me] a discerning heart . . . to distinguish between right and wrong."

Because He invites us to ask, we can rest in the knowledge that God is pleased to answer our prayer.

Uncommon Power

God delights to share His insight, wisdom, and guidance with us. Help is only a prayer away.

Praise Prompt

I praise you, God, for inviting us to bring our frailty, confusion, and fears to you. You never scold us for lacking knowledge. Instead, you pour out your wisdom on us. Each time we humble ourselves, acknowledge our need, and seek your wisdom, you graciously respond. I praise you for giving us your Word that contains so much guidance and direction. Thank you for the Holy Spirit who lives inside us, teaching and leading us into all truth.

Live It Out

When you have to make a decision, do you pray first? Last? Or never? Where do you go for wise counsel? The next time you encounter a situation that seems uncertain, pray first. Ask God for wisdom, then look for it in spiritual places.

55

Jehoshaphat's Prayer for Help

**For we have no power to face this vast
army that is attacking us. We do not know
what to do, but our eyes are on you.**

2 CHRONICLES 20:12

Early one morning my friend Cassie dragged herself out of the house to walk the nearby woods. She'd never felt so despondent.

Months earlier her husband had lost his position of twenty years when his company downsized. At first Jim approached his job hunt with purpose and enthusiasm, but as the months dragged by with little success, his spirits sank. He barely moved from the bed to the couch each morning, drowning in a sea of depression.

Cassie tried her best to support him. She posted Scripture verses about God's provision, asked friends to pray, and encouraged Jim's friends to reach out. Each morning she prayed, "God, please let this be the day Jim finds a job."

One morning she invited him to walk with her. "It'll do you good to get out," she pleaded, to no avail. Jim barely acknowledged her. The sight of her usually cheerful husband sitting on the sofa, shoulders slumped, eyes half closed, broke her heart.

"Lord," she prayed as she trudged the leaf-strewn path, "I don't think I can take it anymore. I've done everything I know to do. I've prayed. I've fasted. I've networked. I've tried to encourage him. I've been firm. I've been understanding. I've clung to your promises. I believe you can deliver us from this season of trial, but I don't know how much longer we can survive. Please help us."

Cassie's prayer for deliverance reminds me of another desperate prayer buried deep in the narrative of 2 Chronicles 20.

King Jehoshaphat and the people of Judah faced a grave threat. Three armies marched against them from neighboring Syria (vv. 1–2).

If I'd been Jehoshaphat, I'd have called out the National Guard, blown the ram's horn to marshal the troops, and summoned the Navy SEALs. But that's not what he did.

"Alarmed, Jehoshaphat *resolved to inquire of the* Lord, and he proclaimed a fast for all Judah" (v. 3). Together with the inhabitants of Judah, he sought God's help first.

We can learn from his example when life's circumstances overwhelm us.

First, he joined hands and hearts with those committed to seeking God. They cleansed themselves of sin and set their minds on God by fasting.

Next, King Jehoshaphat acknowledged God's nature—powerful, sovereign, and invincible. "Lord, the God of our ancestors, are you not the God who is in heaven? You rule over all the kingdoms of the nations. Power and might are in your hand, and no one can withstand you" (v. 6).

He testified to God's faithfulness in the past to inspire their trust in Him for the future. "Our God, did you not drive out the inhabitants of this land before your people Israel and give it forever to the descendants of Abraham your friend?" (v. 7).

Then he spelled out the threat. "This vast army . . . is attacking us" (v. 12).

Finally he asked for God's help, acknowledging their helplessness and need for wisdom. "Our God, will you not judge them? For we have no power to face this vast army that is attacking us. We do not know what to do, *but our eyes are on you*" (v. 12).

When they had presented their requests to God, they waited in faith for His response. "All the men of Judah, with their wives and children and little ones, stood there before the LORD" (v. 13).

Through the prophet Jahaziel, God spoke, "Do not be afraid or discouraged because of this vast army. For the battle is not yours, but God's. . . . You will not have to fight this battle. Take up your positions; stand firm and see the deliverance the LORD will give you, Judah and Jerusalem. Do not be afraid; do not be discouraged. Go out to face them tomorrow, and the LORD will be with you" (vv. 15, 17).

At this good word, Jehoshaphat and his people bowed before the Lord and worshipped. The next day, with the choir leading the way, they marched out to meet their enemies, singing "Give thanks to the LORD, for his love endures forever" (v. 21).

God delivered His people that day. He caused all three armies to turn on each other, destroying Israel's enemies even before Judah arrived on the scene.

Cassie and Jim's story ended almost as dramatically. After Cassie had poured out her heart to the Lord, she admitted, "Lord, we don't know what to do, but our eyes are on you." She returned home to find Jim waiting for her on the porch.

"Remember Steve, from the lumber supply company?" he said, talking so fast his words spilled out in a flood. "His division is looking to hire someone, and he recommended me. With my work experience and his recommendation, he says I'm a shoo-in."

Like Jehoshaphat and the people of Judah, Cassie and Jim danced, wept, and lifted their voices in thanksgiving. "Give thanks to the LORD, for his love endures forever."

Uncommon Power

When we don't know what to do, we can call on God for wisdom, direction, and deliverance.

Praise Prompt

Father, I praise you this day for being Lord over every circumstance that touches my life. Nothing enters my world without your fingerprints upon it. Teach me to bring every need I have to you—first, not last—so you can display your might for all to see. Keep my eyes on you and help me rest in confident faith.

Live It Out

Oftentimes we pray last instead of first when we encounter a crisis. Spend time today reading 2 Chronicles 20:1–30 to learn from Jehoshaphat's example.

56

Daniel's Prayer of Repentance

We do not make requests of you
because we are righteous,
but because of your great mercy.

DANIEL 9:18

Most know the biblical Daniel as the Jewish exile who was thrown into the lions' den for defying the king's decree and praying to God. Some may picture him interpreting the handwriting on King Belshazzar's wall. Others remember that he and his teenage friends Shadrach, Meshach, and Abednego risked death for refusing to break Jewish law and eat the king's delicacies.

Daniel's history of biblical integrity while living in a pagan culture shines from the pages of Scripture. His prayer of repentance and mercy in Daniel 9 glows exceptionally bright. Here's a portion of it:

"Lord, the great and awesome God, who keeps his covenant of love with those who love him and keep his commandments, we have sinned and done wrong. We have been wicked and have rebelled;

we have turned away from your commands and laws. We have not listened to your servants the prophets, who spoke in your name to our kings, our princes and our ancestors, and to all the people of the land" (vv. 4–6).

I find it remarkable that Daniel used the words *we* and *us* twenty-four times in his prayer for his nation.

I've never been moved to pray like Daniel did—until recently. Like Daniel, I've served the Lord for decades. I've stayed true to my commitment to follow God and served Him since I was a teenager. I've stood for biblical truth, led people to faith in Christ, and labored to build God's kingdom.

Why, then, would I pray a prayer of abject confession, self-debasement, and guilt-infused repentance?

Why would Daniel?

He didn't live in flagrant rebellion like his countrymen. He didn't disregard biblical principles and flaunt his sin before God and everyone else. By God's grace, neither do I. And neither do you, I suspect.

Yet Daniel identified with his kinsmen. He loved his broken and backslidden neighbors. He grieved for his family, friends, and fellow exiles drinking deeply from the anti-God potion and rushing headlong into destruction. He mourned his nation's faded glory.

Daniel was an Israelite—by blood and by association. For better or for worse, the Jews were his people. God had placed Daniel among them and called him to be a light, a witness, and a prayer warrior. This is why he could pray, in corporate identification, "*We* and our kings, our princes and our ancestors are covered with shame, Lord, because *we* have sinned against you" (v. 8).

Now, more than ever, our country needs our prayers. Like Daniel, we must humble ourselves and seek God's face on behalf of our nation.

But we must repent of *our* sins first—for failing to pray, neglecting to speak out, and turning away our faces while sinful laws and policies stole the rights of the most vulnerable among us. Only then, when *our* hearts are clean, can we advocate on behalf of our nation.

"The Lord our God is merciful and forgiving, even though we have rebelled against him," Daniel prayed, and we can too. "We have not obeyed the Lord our God or kept the laws he gave us through his servants the prophets. All Israel has transgressed your law and turned away, refusing to obey you. Therefore the curses and sworn judgments written in the Law of Moses, the servant of God, have been poured out on us, because we have sinned against you" (vv. 9–11).

Like Daniel, we don't deserve God's deliverance—but we can pray for His mercy.

"We do not make requests of you because we are righteous, *but because of your great mercy*" (v. 18).

God's mercy—His undeserved favor—is our only hope. Like prisoners sentenced to die, we must come before our righteous Judge with broken and contrite hearts. We must fling ourselves at Jesus's nail-pierced feet and beg for the mercy only He can bestow.

"Lord, listen! Lord, forgive! Lord, hear and act! For your sake, my God, do not delay, because your city and your people bear your Name" (v. 19).

Perhaps then God will have mercy on our country—for His sake and for ours.

Uncommon Power

We do not petition God on behalf of our country because we are righteous and deserving but because He is exceedingly merciful.

Praise Prompt

Father God, it is only through your mercy that we can stand before you. We repent of the sins that stain our hands—sins of apathy, selfishness, and self-centeredness. We agree that repentance must begin in our hearts before it can spread to those around us. Hear our cry, O Lord. Call your people to repentance and heal our land.

Live It Out

Do you identify with our nation and her sins, or do you see yourself as set apart because of your faith? Has Daniel's example changed your perspective? Do you believe God can, as He did for the nation of Israel, restore our country if the godly pray for its restoration? Will you begin today to pray for God's mercy?

57

Ezra's Prayer for God's Reputation

I was ashamed to ask the king for soldiers and horsemen to protect us from enemies on the road, because we had told the king, "The gracious hand of our God is on everyone who looks to him."

EZRA 8:22

Have you ever felt like God's reputation was at stake, and it was up to you to defend it? Maybe you spoke boldly to an unbeliever about God's ability to answer prayer, yet now God seems silent about something you've asked Him for. Or you shared with a skeptic how God promises to supply all your needs according to His riches in glory, but now you have an unmet need.

I found myself in this awkward position the summer before my senior year in dental hygiene school. I'd been a Christian less than a year. My faith was new and exciting, and every day was an adventure.

As I read my Bible, I discovered promises about how God provides for His children. I shared them with my classmates, many of whom weren't believers. I desperately wanted them to experience the joy and peace I had in my relationship with God.

One day I got a letter—a letter that said my full-tuition scholarship was ending.

"What am I going to do if I can't finish school?" I wailed to my best friend. "I just told everyone how God provides for His children, and now my scholarship disappears? What are they gonna think about God now?"

Ezra had an even greater mission field than I had in my college years. A scribe in Babylon during Israel's captivity, Ezra had bragged on God to mighty King Artaxerxes.

As he prepared to lead a group of Israel's most prominent citizens back to Jerusalem after the nation's seventy-year captivity, he went with the king's full permission. Not only had Artaxerxes granted Ezra's request to return to Jerusalem as a teacher of the law, he offered to send him back with all the gold and silver needed to outfit the temple.

As Ezra and his compatriots stood poised to begin their journey, he wrestled with conflicting emotions. He felt excited about returning to his native land, yet he was fully aware of the danger that lay ahead of them. So Ezra proclaimed a fast.

I suspect he'd studied the map and knew about the nine hundred miles of rugged terrain between Babylon and Jerusalem. He looked into the eyes of the men, women, and children who trusted him to lead them safely home. He eyed the pile of gold and silver that robbers would eagerly kill for. And he thought about the opportunity for a pagan king and his officials to come to believe in the God of the universe.

"There, by the Ahava Canal, I proclaimed a fast," Ezra wrote, "so that we might humble ourselves before our God and ask him for a safe journey for us and our children, with all our possessions. I was ashamed to ask the king for soldiers and horsemen to protect us from enemies on the road, because we had told the king, 'The gracious hand of our God is on everyone who looks to him, but his great anger is against all who forsake him'" (Ezra 8:21–22).

Ezra had testified to King Artaxerxes that God Almighty was able to meet their needs and carry them safely to Jerusalem. Now it was time for him to step out in faith.

The same was true in my situation. If I believed God had called me to dental hygiene school and could provide what I needed to complete my education, I had to step out in faith.

"Lord," I prayed, "please send the money I need to finish school— not only for my sake, but for my classmates'. They heard me quote your promise that you'd supply all I need according to your riches in glory. They're watching to see if you'll do it. They need to know you're a promise-keeping God." By faith, I registered for the next semester's classes.

Ezra 8:23, 31–32 records the outcome of Ezra's request: "So we fasted and petitioned our God about this, and he answered our prayer . . . On the twelfth day of the first month we set out from the Ahava Canal to go to Jerusalem. The hand of our God was on us, and he protected us from enemies and bandits along the way. So we arrived in Jerusalem."

My story ended on a similarly happy note. A change in federal funding for needy students provided enough money to complete my education and graduate with no debt. When I received the letter from school confirming my financial aid, my classmates and I did a happy dance. God had affirmed His plan for me to continue my education.

We don't know if King Artaxerxes came to believe in the God of Israel, but Ezra's faith-filled words and example gave him solid reasons to do so. My classmates also had the chance to witness God's faithfulness to me and to our other Christian classmates.

At our thirtieth-class reunion, one classmate stood up and said, "I wasn't a Christian when we attended school together, but I watched your lives and listened to your conversations. Your examples paved the way for me to come to faith. Thank you for playing a part in my salvation."

Uncommon Power

When we pray and God answers, we set the stage for others to trust Him.

Praise Prompt

I praise you, Father, for using our frail and faltering examples to point people to you. What an honor to represent you as we walk through this world with you by our side. Show yourself mighty on our behalf so others can see your love and faithfulness displayed in our lives. In the strong name of Jesus I ask, amen.

Live It Out

Have you considered that how we interact with God in prayer affects, at least in part, how others view Him? Who around you is watching you live out your faith? A coworker? Family member? Friend? Child or grandchild? Spouse? Ask God to grow your faith and use you as a credible witness in their lives.

58

Peter's Prayer of Confession

When Simon Peter saw this, he fell at
Jesus' knees and said, "Go away from me,
Lord; I am a sinful man!"

LUKE 5:8

I used to think I was a pretty good person. I obeyed all major laws (traffic violations not withstanding); accurately reported my income to the IRS; and treated animals, children, and the elderly with kindness. I rescued turtles crossing the road and tossed money into the Salvation Army kettle every Christmas.

But something happened during a Good Friday service that changed my perspective forever.

Through the miracle of multimedia I found myself transported to a craggy hill outside Jerusalem. A man, blood-soaked and unrecognizable, struggled to lift a rough-hewn cross.

Only days before, He'd cradled children in His arms, raised dead sons to life, and restored sanity to the demon possessed. He'd commanded His followers to obey the government, pray for their enemies, and give to the poor.

For these crimes and others like them, the Romans wanted to execute Him.

But I knew the real reason He would die.

Those bloody stripes running down His back? They should have been mine. The nails that pierced His feet and hands? They were meant for me. The wrath of God poured out on His sinless soul? I deserved it.

Sitting in the dark sanctuary watching the perfect Son of God executed before my eyes—seeing His agony and hearing His cries—my heart cracked wide open.

"Oh, Lord," I sobbed. "I don't deserve such love. I wasn't worth it."

Tears blurred my vision, but I could still read the verse that appeared on the screen.

"Very rarely will anyone die for a righteous person, though for a good person someone might possibly dare to die. But God demonstrates his own love for us in this: *While we were still sinners*, Christ died for us" (Romans 5:7–8).

While we were still sinners . . .

Peter the disciple had a heart-cracking experience centuries before mine. He'd heard of Christ, perhaps even sat under His teaching. But that day, all he wanted to do was go home. He and his partners had fished all night and caught nothing. Tired, stinky, and disgusted, he was headed for bed as soon as he washed his last net.

Until Jesus commandeered his boat—as a speaking platform, no less.

Peter impatiently eyed the crowd on the shore and the rising sun and longed for sleep. When the teacher concluded His message, Peter picked up his oars to row the boat back to shore. Jesus's words stopped him midstroke.

"Put out into deep water, and let down the nets for a catch" (Luke 5:4).

Words of protest poured from Simon's lips, but something silenced him. Maybe it was the authority with which Jesus spoke. Or His confident promise of a catch. Or the way He looked past Peter's eyes deep into his soul.

Peter shrugged his weary shoulders and sighed, "Because you say so, I will let down the nets."

The deluge of fish that filled his net was nothing compared to the torrent of conviction that flooded his soul. Surrounded by a boatful of evidence, he was sure this was no ordinary teacher. He knew he wasn't worthy to stand in His presence.

Falling to his knees, he prostrated himself at Jesus's feet. "Go away from me, Lord," he cried. "I am a sinful man!"

Whether Peter knew Jesus was God at that moment or not, Scripture doesn't say, but he obviously had a sudden awareness of his own sin and unworthiness. He would later declare, "You are the Messiah, the Son of the living God" (Matthew 16:16).

Our world tells us there's good in everyone. Scripture says otherwise. "There is no one who does good, not even one" (Romans 3:12). Until we fully understand the depth of our sinfulness, we cannot fully appreciate the price Jesus paid to set us free.

That night during the Good Friday service, I learned what Peter had learned in the boat. Only after God cracks open our hearts and shows us what's inside can we fall at His feet in confession, repentance, and gratitude.

Uncommon Power

Being reminded of our need for a Savior can infuse our prayer lives with praise, gratitude, and humility.

Praise Prompt

Oh Father, how great is the love you have lavished on us that we should be called the children of God. I could never earn your love. I certainly don't deserve it, but I am infinitely grateful. May I never forget that my sin caused your death. May I never, ever, take sin lightly. Help me be quick to confess my sin in prayer and express my gratitude to you in thanksgiving. In Jesus's name I pray, amen.

Live It Out

Instead of rushing through today's devotion, spend time picturing the events of Christ's crucifixion. Ponder the high cost of your sin. Reflect on God's great love, demonstrated by His willingness to offer His only Son as a ransom for our sin. If you've never repented of your sin and asked Christ to be your Savior, do it today. If you know Christ as Savior, confess the sin that keeps you from living a sold-out life for Him.

59

Jesus's Prayer
of Surrender

My Father, if it is possible,
may this cup be taken from me.
Yet not as I will, but as you will.

MATTHEW 26:39

When you hear the word *surrender*, what comes to mind? Do you picture two boys wrestling in the dirt until the weaker yields to the stronger and gasps, "I give up"? Perhaps you think of a recent argument with your parents, spouse, or teenager. Despite being fully convinced you're right, you surrender out of sheer exhaustion. Or maybe you recall a scene from an old war movie. After years of battles and bombs, a beleaguered army eyes its mounting death toll and waves the white flag.

Surrender smacks of loss. Of being vanquished, routed, and bested. Those who surrender always lose.

This may be true in the physical world, but not in the spiritual.

Two thousand years ago a terrible war took place in the garden of Gethsemane. Flesh wrestled with Spirit. Humanity wrestled with divinity. Death wrestled with eternal life.

While His disciples slept, Jesus took on the forces of evil in a battle that decided the fate of humanity. He faced the betrayal of His disciples, the agony of the cross, and the repulsive act of shouldering the world's sin. Overwhelmed with sorrow, He wept. He sweated. And He prayed.

"If there's any way," He said to His Father, "let this cup pass from Me." The fully human Son of God cringed at what He knew was coming. He dreaded walking through the valley of the shadow of death. He shuddered at the horror of bearing the sins of the world.

But despite His fully human emotions, the God-man set His face toward Calvary. In the darkness of Gethsemane, He turned His gaze toward heaven and won the victory.

"Not as I will," He prayed, "but as you will."

Author Jennifer Kennedy Dean, in her book, *Live a Praying Life*, calls Jesus's prayer, "the prayer of relinquishment."

> This is not a prayer of resignation to the circumstances; it's not throwing in the towel and giving up. The prayer of relinquishment can only come from a heart that knows the heart of the Father-Shepherd. We can abandon ourselves fully to His will because we know that His heart does not contain one thought or desire toward us that is anything less than the highest possible good.[20]

Christ knew the heart of God because it beat in His chest. He knew from the foundation of the world that God had ordained Him to die as a ransom for mankind. He knew only the offering of a sinless sacrifice and the resurrection of a victorious Savior would wipe the sin slate clean for those who would believe. He rested in the knowledge that a greater good would follow a horrible evil, and an all-encompassing joy would replace a gut-wrenching grief.

And so, as He had every day of His life, Christ surrendered His will to the Father's.

There He won the victory.

Hours before He died on the cross and days before He rose again, Jesus triumphed over the forces of death, hell, and Satan. By surrendering to God's perfect plan, He routed the world's greatest enemies and redeemed mankind. His submission made it possible for us to live forever with Him in heaven.

Every time we yield our will to God's as Jesus did, we gain a victory. Our yes doesn't save the world. Jesus has already done that. Our surrender aligns us with God's purposes and advances His work. When we obey His Word, we become accurate representatives of God before others. When we trust God to use what He hates to accomplish what He loves, we demonstrate what genuine faith looks like. When we cling to biblical truth while the world laughs, we stand for right even when it costs us.

The longer I live, the more I realize the Christian life is a series of surrenders. And every surrender to the perfect will of God is a victory.

Uncommon Power

When we pray the true prayer of surrender, God will help us overcome our deepest fears by His presence and power. He will enable us to surrender our will to His in faith and trust.

Praise Prompt

Father, I praise you for the mighty victory you accomplished through Jesus's willing and humble surrender. We don't deserve the kind of love He lavished upon us—that we should be called children of God! Give me the faith to walk in His footsteps as I lay down my life for you and those around me.

Live It Out

Have you ever prayed the "prayer of relinquishment"? What did God do through your faith-filled (and perhaps frightened) surrender? Keep in mind that sometimes God doesn't allow us to see the results of our obedience until we get to heaven. Is there something about which you need to pray the prayer of relinquishment? Identify what's holding you back, and trust God with it today.

60

John's Prayer for the Bridegroom

Even so, come, Lord Jesus!

REVELATION 22:20 (NKJV)

Katie was twenty-eight years old when she was diagnosed with multiple sclerosis. Her symptoms developed gradually. First she noticed numbness and weakness on the left side of her body. Then she experienced visual disturbances. When one leg began to drag, it became obvious even to the casual observer that something was seriously wrong.

She met Matt at the gym where she worked out on good days. He says her determination and grit attracted him first, but if you press him, he'll admit it was her wide blue eyes and sweet smile that lingered in his mind day after day.

Within six months, they were dating. A year later, Matt proposed. Although their love grew stronger, Katie's body grew weaker. Two months before their wedding day, she set aside the leg braces and crutches that had helped her walk and transitioned to a wheelchair.

Normally upbeat, Katie couldn't hold back tears.

"I've always imagined *walking* down the aisle on my wedding day, not rolling," she said with a wobbly grin, "but my body just won't cooperate."

On the day of their wedding, Matt stood at the front of the church, eager for a glimpse of his bride. The music swelled, the guests stood, and the door to the narthex swung open.

There Katie sat, just as he had pictured her a thousand times, stunningly beautiful and smiling. His eyes filled with tears and his throat tightened as their eyes met. Behind her stood her father, straight and proud, preparing to roll his baby girl down the aisle.

But before he could move, Katie gripped the armrests, pushed herself up, and stood. She took one tentative step, then another, her eyes fixed on her bridegroom.

But then she wavered. And faltered. And would have fallen if Matt hadn't closed the distance between them and scooped her up in his strong arms. With a face-splitting grin and a whoop of celebration, he marched to the altar and stood before the pastor, cradling his beloved bride to his chest.

"Do you, Matt, take Katie to be your wedded wife . . ."

John the apostle, exiled on the Isle of Patmos, witnessed a wedding—a heavenly wedding. A wedding that is yet to come. Listen to his description:

"I heard what sounded like a great multitude, like the roar of rushing waters and like loud peals of thunder, shouting, 'Hallelujah! For our Lord God Almighty reigns. Let us rejoice and be glad and give him glory! For the wedding of the Lamb has come, and his bride has made herself ready'" (Revelation 19:6–7).

On that day, we, the church, the bride of Christ, will stand before our Bridegroom dressed in "fine linen, bright and clean. . . . (Fine linen stands for the righteous acts of God's holy people)" (v. 8). He'll gather us to His side, and together we'll stand before the Father's altar. There, in the presence of many witnesses, Christ will pledge His undying love to us.

"I, Jesus, take thee, my bride, to love, honor, and cherish for all eternity."

Then the celebration will begin and never stop. "Blessed are those," John wrote, "who are invited to the wedding supper of the Lamb!" (v. 9).

A banquet table sagging under the weight of a thousand delicacies will stretch before us. The holiest and most ethereal music will fill our ears. David will play his harp. Angels will sound their trumpets. A choir of cherubim will join us as we sing the song of the saints.

"Holy, holy, holy is the LORD Almighty; the whole earth is full of his glory . . . You are worthy, our Lord and God, to receive glory and honor and power, for you created all things, and by your will they were created . . . Hallelujah! For our Lord God Almighty reigns. Let us rejoice and be glad and give him glory!" (Isaiah 6:3; Revelation 4:11; 19:6–7).

We'll bow at Jesus's feet, raise our hands to His throne, and shout for joy as the hurt, pain, and fears of a lifetime melt in His presence.

"And behold, I am coming quickly, and My reward is with Me," our Bridegroom promises. "And the Spirit and the bride say, 'Come!' And let him who hears say, 'Come!' And let him who thirsts come. Whoever desires, let him take the water of life freely . . . 'Surely I am coming quickly'" (Revelation 22:12, 17, 20 NKJV).

As we wait for that day, let us join our voices with John's and pray the prayer of the saints throughout the ages.

"Even so, come, Lord Jesus!"

Uncommon Power

One day Jesus, our Bridegroom, will come to claim us as His bride, and we will live with Him forever. We long for that day, and as we wait, we pray, "Come quickly, Lord Jesus!"

Praise Prompt

Oh Father! What a day that will be when you tell Jesus, "Go and get your bride." When I think that you chose us—fallen, sinful people—as your beloved, my heart cannot contain the gratitude and praise that wells up inside me. Unlike earthly husbands, you'll never fail me. You'll never leave me or forsake me. Your steadfast love endures forever.

Live It Out

Have you ever imagined what the marriage supper of the Lamb will look like? Have you pictured yourself as part of the bride of Christ, standing in spotless robes, radiant and pure before God? Imagine this for a moment. How should this future reality affect how we live and pray now? Read 2 Corinthians 11:2, Revelation 19:7–8, and Matthew 25:1–13 for glimpses of how we can prepare for that day.

Acknowledgments

Every time a publisher entrusts me with the privilege of creating a book, I feel a bit like King David. When God announced through Nathan the prophet that He would choose David's son Solomon to build the Lord's temple in Jerusalem, David went in and sat before the Lord and said, "Who am I, Sovereign LORD, and what is my family, that you have brought me this far?" (2 Samuel 7:18).

Who am I?

- Wife to Pastor/Hubby David for almost forty years (I was a child bride)
- Mom to two amazing women and their kind husbands
- Gigi to four wise and wonderful grandchildren and one adorable Frenchie
- A registered dental hygienist for almost forty years (my day job and endless source of material)
- A happy transplant from charming-yet-cold Bristol, Rhode Island, to equally-charming-but-much-less-cold Lexington, South Carolina
- Who has written part of every book (so far) in the mountains of North Carolina, which I consider almost heaven (sorry, John Denver)

- And who loves ice cream and scalding hot baths (not at the same time), sunshine, walks, and snuggling with warm puppies and grandchildren. An ideal day would be spent at the beach or mountains with my family, surrounded by my grandchildren and grandpuppy, reading to them while they listened enraptured. If there was a tub of Maple Walnut ice cream or Trader Joe's Dark Chocolate Covered Almonds with Sea Salt nearby, all the better.

These facts give you a snapshot of me, but perhaps the weightiest truth about me is that I am who I am by God's grace. I'm fully aware that writing and speaking for God is an honor, a privilege, and a weighty responsibility. I couldn't do it without those He has gathered by my side:

My husband, David, is my theological sounding board and greatest encourager. If he didn't love me, I doubt I could form a single coherent thought, much less dig deeply into the mysteries of God.

Dawn Anderson from Our Daily Bread Publishing, who was brave enough to take a chance on me. I am forever grateful.

Bob Hostetler, my wise and kind agent, who also took a chance on me (not that you had a choice), and Les Stobbe, my first agent, who had a choice but did it anyway. I'm doing my best to make you proud (and buy you a meal now and then).

Rachel Kirsch, my ODB editor who polished my manuscript and pushed me to dig deeper and write clearer. I'm grateful for you, in an exhausted kind of way.

Jean Wilund, my critique partner, prayer partner, and best writing buddy. You are God's gift to me. Your eagle-eyed critiques, unceasing prayers, and unwavering support make everything I write better. Thank you for knowing when to pull my work out of the fire and when to stand beside me and feed it into the flames.

Jeannie, Julie, Jean, and Lisa, the Monketeers; and my Lexington Word Weavers critique group—y'all aren't colleagues, you're family, and I love you.

Steve Bradley, Debbie DeCiantis, Dawn Gonzalez, Mary Huffman, Lisa Kent, Don and Debbie McCutcheon, Debbie Melton, Don Sarazen, Linnea Shick, Mike and Jean Sutton, Mandy Smith, and Debbie Watford—my beta reader team. Thank you so much for sharing your thoughts, insight, and prayers.

Kristen, Michael, Mary Leigh, Josiah, Lauren, Caroline, Andrew, Collin, and Halsey—my family. My love for you and my desire to see God fulfill His good purposes for your lives pushes me to grow deeper and wider in my prayer life.

Robert and Lillian Slice, my parents. Without you, I wouldn't be living this joy-filled life. I love you so much.

And you. Thanks so much for reading. If *Refresh Your Prayers* has blessed you, would you be so kind as to leave your honest review online at Our Daily Bread Publishing, Goodreads, Amazon, or wherever you purchase books? I'd be most grateful.

—Lori

Notes

1. Catherine Marshall, *A Man Called Peter: The Story of Peter Marshall* (Grand Rapids, MI: Chosen Books, 1951), 348, 352.

2. C. S. Lewis, *The C. S. Lewis Signature Classics* (New York: HarperOne, 2017), 461.

3. Frank Laubach, *The Game with Minutes* (Eastford, CT: Martino Fine Books, 2012).

4. Unknown, July 6, 2021, comment on Lori Hatcher, "When Is It OK to Stop Praying?" *Hungry for God, Starving for Time* (blog), October 15, 2017, https://lori-benotweary.blogspot.com/2017/10/when-is-it-ok-to -stop-praying.html#comment-form.

5. Oswald Chambers, *Christian Disciplines* (Grand Rapids, MI: Discovery House, 1995), 130–131.

6. Jennifer Kennedy Dean, *Live a Praying Life: Open Your Life to God's Power and Provision* (Birmingham, AL: New Hope, 2010), 39.

7. "Seven Spurgeon Quotes for Those Who Carry Burdens," *The Spurgeon Center* (blog), October 18, 2016, https://www.spurgeon.org/resource -library/blog-entries/7–spurgeon-quotes-for-those-who-carry-burdens/.

8. Andrew Murray, *Waiting on God* (self-pub., CreateSpace, 2017), 66.

9. William Law, *A Serious Call to a Devout and Holy Life* (Philadelphia: Westminster Press, 1990), 135.

10. Charles H. Spurgeon, "January 13: Never Cast Out," in *Faith's Check-book*, https://archive.spurgeon.org/fcb/fcb-bod.htm.

11. Mason Locke Weems, *The Life of Washington* (New York: M. E. Sharpe, 1996), 10.

12. "Paul's Thorn in the Flesh," Blue Letter Bible, accessed June 8, 2021, https://www.blueletterbible.org/faq/thorn.cfm.

13. *Strong's Concordance*, s.v. "paraklétos," accessed July 13, 2021, https ://biblehub.com/greek/3875.htm.

14. The Bible does not name Eliezer in Genesis 24, but most Bible scholars agree that he would have been the servant chosen by Abraham. See "Who Was Eliezer in the Bible?" Got Questions, accessed July 7, 2021, https://www.gotquestions.org/Eliezer-in-the-Bible.html.

15. Franklin Graham, *Billy Graham in Quotes* (Nashville: Thomas Nelson, 2011), 155.

16. J. Sidlow Baxter, quoted in Cameron V. Thompson, *Master Secrets of Prayer* (Guatemala: Service of Life Schools), 4.

17. "2021 World Watch List Report," Open Doors USA, accessed June 1, 2021, https://www.opendoorsusa.org/2020–world-watch-list-report/.

18. The Voice of the Martyrs. Accessed November 4, 2021. https://www .persecution.com/.

19. Elisabeth Elliot, *Love Has a Price Tag* (Chappaqua, NY: Christian Herald Books, 1979), 96.

20. Dean, *Live a Praying Life*, 162.

Help us get the word out!

Our Daily Bread Publishing exists to feed the soul with the Word of God.

If you appreciated this book, please let others know.

- Pick up another copy to give as a gift.
- Share a link to the book or mention it on social media.
- Write a review on your blog, on a bookseller's website, or at our own site (odb.org/store).
- Recommend this book for your church, book club, or small group.

Connect with us:

 @ourdailybread

@ourdailybread

 @ourdailybread

Our Daily Bread Publishing
PO Box 3566
Grand Rapids, Michigan 49501 USA

✉ books@odb.org